All of humanity carries the im[...] God has "named" his children with dignity—so that we might flourish and empower others to flourish. In *Known*, church planter and author Aubrey Sampson invites the reader to embrace his or her true "name" in Jesus so that the Name above every other name will be honored by all. Read this book and know the name above all others.

DR. DERWIN L. GRAY, lead pastor of Transformation Church, author of *God, Do You Hear Me?*

So many of us struggle with insecurity and unworthiness because we take our cues for value from what we see around us. *Known* helps us redirect our vision to the only place that matters: the Word of God. This book is like God calling us on the phone to remind us who we are in him. I pray many discover the truth in these words.

NONA JONES, bestselling author of *Success from the Inside Out*, head of global faith-based partnerships at Facebook

There are a lot of voices shouting at us about who we are. *Known* cuts through the noise with the biblical truths about how God sees us. Experience the powerful reality of God's personal and specific names for you. Read this book, and you'll find yourself freed and empowered to bless a hurting world.

MARK BATTERSON, *New York Times* bestselling author of *The Circle Maker*, lead pastor of National Community Church

In *Known*, Aubrey Sampson bravely shines a light on both our individual and communal pain. At the same time, she points us to a greater truth: God has specific and powerful names that counter every lie about who we are. What an invitation—to know how God sees us and loves us and to offer a hurting world an identity that can never be shaken.

DR. ANITA PHILLIPS, LCSW-C, trauma therapist, host of *In the Light* podcast

If you ever wanted to explore your identity and family name as a child of God, this is the book to pick up. In such a personal, authentic, vulnerable (yet biblical) way, Aubrey emphatically and comprehensively declares how you are known by God. My prayer as you read *Known*: Not only will you come to know who God says you to be, but you (as the title says) will come to believe who God says you are—and that, my friends, will change everything, from how you live to how you live sent.

ED STETZER, executive director of Wheaton College Billy Graham Center

Aubrey's book could be read slowly over time, but I ended up reading it in one sitting because I just couldn't get enough. Her words are powerful but always kind and tender. I loved the way she made deep theological truths and stellar exegetical work accessible and relevant to any of us struggling to find our identity in Christ. After two decades of teaching the Bible, I know this resource should be in the hands of any Christian seeking more intimacy with Christ.

KAT ARMSTRONG, author of *No More Holding Back* and *The In-Between Place*, preacher, cofounder of The Polished Network

There is a cosmic battle being waged for the identity of every one of us. In *Known: How Believing Who God Says You Are Changes Everything*, my friend Aubrey Sampson does a masterful job exposing the lies and telling us the truth about our true identity in God. Sampson addresses one of the great contemporary questions of our time in an insightful, challenging, and compelling fashion. Read *Known* for yourself, but then share it with a friend.

DAVE FERGUSON, lead pastor of Community Christian Church, author of *B.L.E.S.S.: 5 Everyday Ways to Love Your Neighbor and Change the World*

Identity is *the* pain point of this generation. Many are risking everything to find who they are. The reality is we can't make an identity, nor can we find one by looking within—it must be given to us by God. But this journey of knowing who we are by God is not just cerebral, it's one that we have to feel in our bones. It has to make sense to us emotionally. This is why Aubrey's book is so wonderful and needed. I was deeply moved as I read her words. She takes the truth of who God says we are and doesn't just put a bow in it. Rather, she takes the reader on a journey that makes us feel all the feels and know what it's like in our messy world to be Known by the only Voice that matters.

DAVID LOMAS, pastor at Reality SF, author of *The Truest Thing About You*

I think every heart on the planet has gotten pretty banged up the past few years, bruised and rubbed raw, buried under layer upon layer of anxieties and insecurities. Then comes the gentle, healing message of *Known*. Author and pastor Aubrey Sampson invites us to come as we are and reminds us that in our most broken places, we are known and named by God.

CATHERINE MCNIEL, author of *Fearing Bravely, All Shall Be Well,* and *Long Days of Small Things*

This book is beautiful. The writing is beautiful, of course, but even more beautiful is the grace Aubrey Sampson writes about. Most beautiful still is the God of grace at the center of this story. This book will encourage you to rest in Jesus and his goodness.

In a time of sorrow and fear, this book steps in to point us to hope: hope in Christ as he sees and loves us.

MICAH FRIES, director of engagement at GlocalNet, director of programs at Multi-Faith Neighbors Network, author of *Leveling the Church*

"What's in a name?" So much more than we (or Shakespeare) might realize. With her usual wit and insight, Aubrey Sampson teaches us that our names are a way of being known and that the name God gives us is the most important one of them all. With Aubrey as a guide, you'll find the courage and freedom to live out of your true self, the one that is known and named by God.

MITCHEL LEE, lead pastor of Grace Community Church

In an age where you can be known by many and yet truly known by none, our souls long to be seen—flaws and all—and chosen nonetheless. In this raw, honest, and brilliant work, Aubrey Sampson shows us how to shed the false names we've assumed for ourselves and rest in the adoption of the Name above all names. I highly recommend this book to anyone who longs to feel completely understood and loved—which is all of us.

DAVEY BLACKBURN, author, speaker, host of the *Nothing Is Wasted* podcast

Aubrey Sampson is a wise teacher, a gentle guide into the tender spaces of our stories. *Known* speaks to our most fundamental longings with transformative hope. May the truths in these pages cause your heart to soar.

ANN VOSKAMP, *New York Times* bestselling author of *The Broken Way* and *One Thousand Gifts*

KNOWN

KNOWN

How Believing
Who God Says You Are
Changes Everything

Aubrey Sampson

Foreword by CHRISTINE CAINE

NavPress

A NavPress resource published in alliance
with Tyndale House Publishers

NavPress ◑

NavPress is the publishing ministry of The Navigators, an international Christian organization and leader in personal spiritual development. NavPress is committed to helping people grow spiritually and enjoy lives of meaning and hope through personal and group resources that are biblically rooted, culturally relevant, and highly practical.

For more information, visit NavPress.com.

Known: How Believing Who God Says You Are Changes Everything

Copyright © 2021 by Aubrey Sampson. All rights reserved.

A NavPress resource published in alliance with Tyndale House Publishers

NavPress and the NavPress logo are registered trademarks of NavPress, The Navigators, Colorado Springs, CO. *Tyndale* is a registered trademark of Tyndale House Ministries. Absence of ® in connection with marks of NavPress or other parties does not indicate an absence of registration of those marks.

The Team:
David Zimmerman, Publisher; Caitlyn Carlson, Acquisitions Editor; Elizabeth Schroll, Copy Editor; Olivia Eldredge, Operations Manager; Eva Winters, Designer

Cover photograph of abstract watercolor copyright © Alison Winterroth/Stocksy. All rights reserved.

Author photograph copyright © 2021 by Lexi Russell. All rights reserved.

Published in association with Tawny Johnson of Illuminate Literary Agency, an Author Management Company. www.illuminateliterary.com.

Some of the anecdotal illustrations in this book are true to life and are included with the permission of the persons involved. All other illustrations are composites of real situations, and any resemblance to people living or dead is purely coincidental.

For information about special discounts for bulk purchases, please contact Tyndale House Publishers at csresponse@tyndale.com, or call 1-855-277-9400.

ISBN 978-1-64158-308-4

Printed in the United States of America

27	26	25	24	23	22	21
7	6	5	4	3	2	1

For Jenn (a name with two n's)—

Your courageous battle with breast cancer

has displayed the ever-increasing glory of God

in ways more powerful than this book ever could.

On Wednesdays, we wear camo.

CONTENTS

FOREWORD
Unnamed

2508 OF 1966.

That's what my birth certificate says. The hospital assigned me a number. Because my mother didn't name me.

Numbers are numbing. They don't feel. They don't see. They don't taste. They don't touch. They don't smell. They don't talk. They don't hear. They don't smile. They don't cry. They don't suffer. They don't live. They don't eat. They don't breathe. They don't desire. Numbers numb.

Numbers are desensitizing. As I'm writing this, there are 40 million slaves in the world.[1] There are 8,500 children dying of hunger every day.[2] There are almost 26 million refugees scattered around the globe.[3] There are 60,000 dead because of natural disasters in the past year.[4] Close to 800,000 have died of suicide.[5] More than 40 million children have been abused.[6] More than 2.5 million have died from COVID-19, and the number is still rising.[7] More than 600,000 have died from breast cancer.[8] When it's a number like these, it's impersonal. Distant. Overwhelming. A statistic. Not a person. But when it's someone you love. Someone you know. Someone who is your mother, sister, wife, daughter, or friend— then it's one too many. Then it's a person, not a number.

Numbers are dehumanizing. When the Jews, Poles, Roma, and Soviet POWs, along with twenty-five thousand other ethnicities, were rounded up and sent to Auschwitz, a number was tattooed on one of their arms. They were no longer regarded as human. No longer someone. No longer anyone. They were just a number. The next number in line for a meager portion of bread. The next number in line to work unrelenting hours. The next number in line to be shot. The next number in line for the pile. They were regarded as dispensable. Usable. Until they no longer were. They were manipulated. Violated. Discarded. Disposed. Incinerated.

My parents who adopted me never called me by the number assigned to me. They called me Christine, which means "follower of Christ." Over time I became exactly what my name meant, but it wasn't until I was thirty-three that I learned I was adopted. I lived more than three decades before I discovered I wasn't who I thought I was. The day I finally held my birth certificate in one hand, with the number 2508 on it, I held a Bible in the other. It was open to Isaiah 49:1 (csb): "The Lord called me before I was born. He named me while I was in my mother's womb."

Names matter to God. It took me a long time to believe that God had named me in my mother's womb because, in addition to being adopted, I grew up a survivor of sexual abuse. And I was marginalized as a young person because of my Greek ethnicity and my gender. It was painful to not feel seen, or known, or accepted, or wanted, or chosen, or loved for so many reasons. I was riddled with shame, fear, insecurity, guilt, anger, bitterness, and broken-ness. I felt like that number on my birth certificate, not a person created in the image of God on purpose and for a purpose.

It was only when I truly encountered Jesus and discovered what he said about me that the trajectory of my life changed. As Aubrey so beautifully pens in this book, it took time to understand . . .

God has named you. You are fully known, exquisitely loved, and securely held in his arms. He has given you names out of who you are now and for who you are in the process of becoming. But God doesn't bring you into this knowledge for knowledge's sake alone or even for your personal transformation alone. He doesn't just give you all the information about your identity, doesn't just tell you all the truths about yourself so you can sit there quietly and stare out at the water.

We are named to *go and live out our names.* We are called to live as "sent ones" on God's mission into the world.

Throughout *Known*, Aubrey poignantly shows the vital necessity of understanding that we are not what happened to us or what we have done. We are not what was said to us or what others have said about us. We are who God says we are, which is why one of the most important journeys we will ever take on this planet is the journey to discover who we really are in Christ. If we know who we are and why we are here, we will live out of that truth and not the facts of our past history or present circumstances. It is only the truth we know that will set us free.

Aubrey has given us a gift in these pages. Prepare to discover the magnificent truth of who you really are. Prepare to discover what God really thinks about you. His love is greater than you have ever imagined. If you live from the truth that you are fully seen, fully known, and fully loved by God, then you will thrive and flourish in life.

Christine Caine
founder of A21 and Propel Women
2021

AS WE BEGIN

A Question

WHAT IS YOUR NAME?

Aubrey, the name my parents gave me, comes from a character in a book and a song by the 1970s band Bread. Each summer, I'd spend a few weeks in the blazing Texas sun at my grandparents' house, and on the first day of my arrival, my sweet Papa would announce my entrance by playing "Aubrey" on his record player. He'd turn up the volume, then sway back and forth, while serenading me as I walked through the door—"And Aubrey was her name, a not so very ordinary girl or name. But who's to blame?"[1]

It still makes me smile to think about my grandpa in red suspenders and starched blue jeans, standing by his record player, filled with giddy anticipation as he waited for the perfect moment to place the needle on the record.

This always felt like a twofold miracle—that my name was actually in a song and that someone I adored knew the words. I heard that song's refrain in my grandpa's tenor and knew immediately that I was welcomed, that I belonged, that I was not only loved but also cherished. I still play it on my own record player every time I miss him.

Depending on where you do your naming research, "Aubrey"

means "elf leader."[2] Or "rules with elf wisdom."[3] My mom, however, rejects the elf etymology altogether and tells me that she chose Aubrey because she read somewhere that it means, simply, "leader with wisdom." I certainly prefer that interpretation as an adult. But as a young girl, I used to play under the weeping willow in my parent's backyard and pretend that I was the long-lost ruler of a hidden tribe of tiny, magical elven folk. My understanding of my name expanded my imagination of myself and helped me envision my place in the world, albeit a fanciful one.

Our names can inspire us, giving us permission to be ourselves.

In the ancient world, a person's name was synonymous with their reputation,[4] and still today, our names in many ways dictate who we will become. Perhaps you were named by doting parents who pored over baby books, discovering the perfect one just for you. Maybe you inherited a family or ancestral name—something strong and rooted in deep meaning. Our names have the potential to help us know who we belong to and that we belong somewhere at all.

Our names can hold a certain authority, strength, and purpose.

Of course, we know that is not true of every birthname. Some of us have traumatic name stories—we feel a sense of pain about our name because our family rejected us, and we carry a real or metaphorical sense of being unwanted. Maybe you don't really know where your name comes from. Maybe it's the vestige of a parent you never knew, or your family never spoke about its meaning. Maybe you have been forced to change your name due to a painful or scary life circumstance.

Our names can have the power to be badges of honor or badges of heartache.

Adding to this emotional complexity, our names are not limited to the ones we're given at birth. We name or define ourselves in other ways, as well—by our jobs, marital statuses, roles, cultural contexts, ethnicities, Enneagram numbers, strengths, talents, spiritual gifts, religious affiliations, tribes, hobbies. Those are wonderful characteristics about us, but even those names are only part of the complex tapestry of who we are and how God made us. They are not the whole of us.

Many of us also carry painful, damaging names that often leave us feeling alone, unknown. Names that we have spoken over ourselves or that others have branded us with—harmful nicknames and false monikers we have lived under, hurtful labels about who we are, lies about our worth and our place in the world. Some of these names loom larger than we want them to, and others aren't always obvious; they exist as fading marks. Scars, stitches, and scratches, barely visible on the surface anymore but regular reminders of our old wounds, difficult stories, and arduous battles.

If you are wearing a name that's been spoken over you, or one that you've held onto for reasons you don't understand anymore— if, as podcaster and author Emily P. Freeman says, you have a name that's "loud enough to have an impact, but not so loud that you remember to turn it off"—my prayer as you read this book is that the Spirit of God will gently, yet mightily, embolden you to leave that name behind.[5]

At the end of the day, only God has the power to name every part of you. His names for you speak the definitive truth over all the other ways you name yourself or the ways you have been named.

What if, in place of the negative names in your story, God wants to speak a new name, a better name, a healing name, a loving name, a freeing name over you? And what if he already has? In God, you are named—perfectly and truly—because in him, you are known completely.

What's at stake for understanding our sacred namedness is nothing less than how we reflect God in the world, how we treat others, and how we allow others to treat us. This concept shapes the very nature of how we live, how we love, how we move and have our being, and how we bear witness to the gospel. Knowing our names, knowing how God sees us and loves us in all of the uniqueness of how he's created us, is foundational to our existence.

This Is Your Name

In these pages, we're going to take a journey into the truth of how you've been named, exploring who you are, whose you are, and how living into those identities changes everything. Each of the chapters calls out one of God's names for you: Beloved, Known, Whole, God's Child, Living Statue, and more. Inspired from various Scriptures about the image of God and the names of God, each of these names proclaims a truth over your life, grounding you in a reality that cannot be shaken:

> Then God said, "Let us make human beings in our image, to be like us. They will reign over the fish in the sea, the birds in the sky, the livestock, all the wild animals on the earth, and the small animals that scurry along the ground."
>
> So God created human beings in his own image.
>   In the image of God he created them;
>   male and female he created them.
>
> Then God blessed them. . . . God looked over all he had made, and he saw that it was very good!
>
> GENESIS 1:26-28, 31, NLT

O Lord, our Lord, your majestic name fills the earth!
  Your glory is higher than the heavens. . . .

What are mere mortals that you should think about them,
  human beings that you should care for them?
Yet you made them only a little lower than God
  and crowned them with glory and honor.

PSALM 8:1, 4-5, NLT

For you created my inmost being;
  you knit me together in my mother's womb.
I praise you because I am fearfully and wonderfully made.

PSALM 139:13-14

All of us who have had that veil removed can see and
reflect the glory of the Lord. And the Lord—who is
the Spirit—makes us more and more like him as we are
changed into his glorious image.

2 CORINTHIANS 3:18, NLT

Put on your new nature, created to be like God—truly
righteous and holy.

EPHESIANS 4:24, NLT

You are a chosen people. You are royal priests, a holy
nation, God's very own possession. As a result, you can
show others the goodness of God, for he called you out of
the darkness into his wonderful light.

  "Once you had no identity as a people;
    now you are God's people.

> Once you received no mercy;
>> now you have received God's mercy."
>
> 1 PETER 2:9-10, NLT

Knowing who we really are is vital to our individual flourishing and our community's flourishing as well. This topic of namedness is crucial to consider in groups, where we can create safe spaces to be vulnerable with one another, speak true names over each other, and point out where we might be living under false names. For that reason, at the end of this book, I've included a study guide and series of questions for personal reflection or small-group/missional-community/book-club discussion. I would highly recommend reading and reflecting on this book with a community of people and/or inviting others into a book study that you lead.

An Invitation

Spiritual director and CEO Ruth Haley Barton suggests that we are always being "saved from who we are not and called to be who we are."[6] As you read, my biggest dream for you is to find freedom from any false name you are living under so that you can simultaneously experience divine transformation, becoming who you truly are in Christ.

This journey to understand who you are, whose you are, and what it all means cannot be embarked on lightly. You are about to peer into the very depths of your soul—the pain you carry, the lies you've believed, the truth that is stronger, and the fundamental worthiness of who God says you are.

So I invite you to take your birthname, its origins, and all the good ways you name yourself—all of the grace-filled and powerful memories of your name—in one hand. Then, carefully and tenderly, take the false or negative names you have been called or have lived under in the other. Together, let's open our hands and present them all before God.

> *God, we are laying our names—both true and false—on a proverbial table before you without judgment. What is your invitation? What new name(s) might you want to speak over us in these pages? What names do you want us to let go of forever? We want to hear our true names from you, oh God, our Namer. Meet us here, will you? For the sake of your name and your glory.*

I asked you a question as we began—*What is your name?* But as we begin, that's actually not the question we need to answer. What matters above all else is this: *Where is your name?* Scripture tells us,

- God has called you by name (Isaiah 43:1).
- Your name is engraved on God's hand (Isaiah 49:16).
- Your name is written in God's Book of Life (Luke 10:20).

That means your name exists in three astonishing places. Your name lives, permanently and perpetually, on the lips of God, in the hand of God, and has poured forth from the pen of God, onto the pages of God.

No matter how false names may have tried to own you, you belong to the One who has named you—the One who has sung the song of your name across time, space, and history. Listen to his voice and live.

Aubrey

PART I

WHO YOU ARE

The names that God calls you are the
only ones you should be answering to.

PRISCILLA SHIRER

THIS IS THE UNIVERSAL HUMAN LONGING: TO BE KNOWN.

Not famous. Not noteworthy. But to be *intimately understood.* We want to know that someone sees us, gets us, accepts us, and is *for* us, just as we are for others. We want to know that the aching and raw places in our souls, the questions we have about our existence, the secret dreams and heartaches we hold, are carefully tended to.

And what we're really longing for—in all of this—is love.

The greatest miracle to ever occur is that the God of the universe knows you and wants to be known by you and has called you by name, as deep calls to deep, into his perfect love.

But who are you in God's sight? He has bestowed on you powerful, loving, and life-changing names—so that you can begin to understand just how *known* you truly are.

BELOVED

Did God Really Say?

Then God blessed them. . . .
God looked over all he had made,
and he saw that it was very good!

GENESIS 1:28, 31, NLT

> The power that brought the swirling stars, the dazzling
> snow, the summer sunrises, and the entire cosmos into
> existence; the power that put on flesh, bore a cross, and
> conquered death and evil—that same power breathed a
> name from the breadth of his unending love for you. It is
> your first name and your truest name: *Beloved*.

DO YOU BELIEVE YOURSELF WORTHY OF LOVE?

My forehead is pressed against a cool airplane window, the
pressure of which is relieving my nausea and mercifully prevent-
ing me from vomiting. Getting sick in one of those small, white
barf bags is an unacceptable option right now, especially because I
am sitting next to a guy who, just a few seconds ago, dumped me.

We've been dating almost a year, and just before this weekend
getaway with our little group of friends, he told me that he loved
me . . . *wait for it* . . . for my potential.

"I love you, for your potential."

Literally. He said this.

What, in fact, he means by this (and I know because he explains it) is that if I begin educating myself on meaningful authors and thoughtful art-house movies, if I can finally improve my taste in music and just sort of generally see the world through different lenses (*his* lenses, I'm guessing)—an education he is willing to undertake—then I will be worthy of his love. He mentions that I should consider a bit more exercise as well.

"One day, I could totally see myself falling in love with you . . . when you are ready for me."

The pitiful thing is that I just sort of blindly accepted this dangling-carrot dynamic of affection for a time. That is, until this flight. (*Sweet Jesus, thank you for this flight!*) It is here on this airplane that I finally realize what a twisted mess the whole situation is.

And it's not like you think. It's not that I look down out of the airplane window at the world below me and come to some profound realization that if he doesn't love me for who I am, then *shame on him*! It's not some empowering moment of self-actualization. It's actually because of a burrito.

Let me explain.

The flight attendant is handing out burritos for the in-flight meal, and the guy keeps going on and on about it. I mean, he Can't. Let. It. Go. He's sitting there in his aisle seat, legs spread out, taking up way too much space as it is. He's got a highlighter stuck behind one ear, and he's reading some pretentious book, but he keeps setting the book down on the tray table in front of him to complain about the *audacity* of burritos on an airplane. "Burritos? What are they thinking! I could *never* eat a burrito on an airplane. It's *sooooo* unappealing. Can you imagine anyone ever deliberately eating that?"

Now, I certainly recognize that airplane burritos might not be the best version of a burrito or the wisest use of tight space and human bodily functions. And the truth is, I don't really even want to eat the airplane burrito, but I also realize that this moment is a watershed for *my entire future.*

I understand that if I don't eat this burrito right this second, I will inadvertently allow myself to remain stuck in this inequitable relationship. I also recognize that this moment isn't truly about *this* guy at all. It's that I suddenly have this new sense of urgency. I don't want to stay trapped in a pattern of desperate dependence on others' approval. I mean, if your entire life's value, your *givenness*, relies on the inconsistent whims of a particular group of people, or on another sinful human being, that is not a great place to be.

So I flag the flight attendant and ask her for a burrito. "Make it a double," I'm tempted to say.

With that, the boyfriend eyeballs me with disbelief and derision, then dumps me. And so with several more uncomfortable hours of flight time to go, my forehead is pressed against the plane's window, not because I am heartbroken over him, and not because I am nauseated by the burrito (it was a good burrito!). But because I am sick to my stomach. I had voluntarily placed myself on a scale of his own making, and in many other ways, on many other occasions, on countless others' scales—frantic to achieve some tenuous measure of worth.

Around this time, I had a mentor who asked me a poignant question: "Do you believe yourself worthy of love?"

I couldn't answer.

Because like so many of us, even before that arrogant boy ever came into the picture, I had named myself falsely. Through the various movements and moments in my life's narrative, up to that point, I had picked up and held on tightly to certain destructive names, names like Rejected, Unworthy, Unlovable, Not Enough.

Ultimately, my mentor was asking a question about my notion of myself in the world. And in doing so, she was saying *that* notion—those false names—desperately needed to be healed.

All of this makes me wonder about you, friend, about your own notions of yourself. Your story may be a tender one—

- A dad who left and never returned.
- A mom whose acceptance you can never quite achieve, no matter how hard you try.
- Violence you've experienced because of your ethnicity or gender.
- A loved one who decided the relationship wasn't worth fighting for, and you're still not sure what you did wrong.
- An identity struggle.
- An inability to measure up to your own standards.
- A long wait for that one big thing to happen—and you're starting to question if it ever will.
- A partner, a friend, the one you thought you would plan with, run with, dream with, and do life with who seems to have moved on without you.
- Another person receiving the attention and acclaim and affirmation you long for, leaving you wondering why you keep getting overlooked.
- A painful sense of abandonment.
- Or a general sense that you can never do enough, be enough, or do it the right way.

"The heart's hunger is infinite," writes author and philosopher James K. A. Smith.[1] And the reality is, our hungry and hurting souls need constant reminders about who we really are.

Even decades after that miserable plane ride—now, when I believe myself to be a settled, empowered, and confident adult— it's astonishing how regularly I catch myself striving, hustling, achieving, posting, earning, doing. Not from joy—from *desperation*. Due to stress or fear or discontentment, or maybe just because I didn't sleep well the night before, I suddenly grow anxious to earn the approval of some ghost, hungry to hit some ever-elusive, ever-blurry target of enoughness.

Whenever that restlessness creeps in, I have to stop and speak grace over myself: "Breathe, little soul. Slow down, little heart. What are you striving for? What are you after? You already have God's approval and love. You are already known and accepted. Be loved, *Beloved*."

Or, borrowing a phrase from King David's own self-talk, "Return to your rest, my soul, for the LORD has been good to you" (Psalm 116:7).

I find this to be such refreshing news. Even the forefathers and foremothers of our faith needed to remind themselves of their true names.

Beloved, Your First Name

The power that brought the swirling stars, the dazzling snow, the summer sunrises, and the entire cosmos into existence; the power that put on flesh, bore a cross, and conquered death and evil—that same power breathed a name from the breadth of his unending love for you. It is your first name and your truest name: *Beloved*.

This name has existed for a long time. Long before the Fall, long before God gave Adam and Eve a tour of their little garden paradise, long before God commissioned them to cultivate the land, or engineer their city, or govern anything—before they *did* anything meaningful or noteworthy—God spoke a blessing of goodness over them, simply because they existed. "You are very good!" God cried out as both a proclamation and a heartfelt response (Genesis 1:31, author's paraphrase).

New Testament scholar and author Scot McKnight writes that "God's glory echoes through all creation: *tov me'od*. Very good! Very well done! Perfect! Harmony! What a masterpiece!" McKnight adds, "All these English terms, and more, are found in the word *tov*."[2]

Over Adam and Eve (and over you, as well), God declares with divine delight, affection, and approval, "You are very good!" And it's not a stretch to assume that "beloved," *agapētos* in Greek—a term that means *special, dear, object of special affection, worthy of love*[3]—is also contained in the Hebrew word *tov*. In fact, in some Bible translations, both terms, *very good* and *beloved*, are similarly defined as "precious."[4]

Which makes sense—these are, after all, statements about the innate value and pleasure that God has for you and feels for you.

It's as if, at the emergence of the created order, God made an announcement about you, a broadcast loud for the entire solar system to hear; God named you with enough force to reach through time and space: *You are very good, my beloved! My beloved, you are very good!*

Ephesians chapter 1 echoes this theme, proclaiming that God chose us in Christ before the creation of the world, "that we should be holy and without blemish before him in love . . . according to the good pleasure of his will, to the praise of the glory of his grace, which he freely bestowed on us in the Beloved" (Ephesians 1:4-6, ASV).

In other words, even *before* that grand announcement, before the foundations of the earth were ever spoken into existence, God was *already* calling you Beloved, through his beloved son, Jesus.

So, when we hear God calling Adam and Eve "very good," we understand that he was simultaneously calling them his dearly loved ones, his beloved children. And what we discover, remarkably, is this: In God's economy, there is no "because" in Beloved. There is no dangling carrot in Beloved. There is no "if you reach your potential" in Beloved.

Though we know that sin will enter the Garden picture and change the narrative, we still need to begin here: with our first name, Beloved. As author and priest Henri Nouwen said, "Self-rejection is the greatest enemy of the spiritual life because it contradicts the sacred voice that calls us the 'Beloved.' Being the Beloved expresses the core truth of our existence."[5]

God's great love for you simply and profoundly *is*, because God is, simply and profoundly, love. God loves you and speaks goodness and delight over you not because you have earned it or achieved it. Because you exist, you are worthy of love.

Did God Really Say . . . ?

Though we are so exquisitely loved by God, this tendency to name ourselves wrongly or to actively live from a place of rejection or unworthiness is an ancient instinct—as old as the Garden of Eden where that primal serpent hissed his subtle question into the universe, into Eve and Adam's ears, and into the echoes of our sacred namedness today: "Did God really say . . . ?"

We tend to think of Satan's craftiness (Genesis 3:1) as shrewd and vile, which is true. But did you know there's another translation for the word *crafty* in Genesis 3? *Crafty* is also *prudent*.[6] As in sensible, as in acting with care and forethought.

Yes, we rightly assign chaos and destruction to the Accuser, and we know where to point the finger when the evil is obvious.

But how often do we fall prey to the enemy's ploys of logic? The serpent is a liar, but don't be fooled; he attacks in ways that are precise, careful. Otherwise we wouldn't fall for them.

Think about the prudence of the question—*Did God really say . . . ?* This is a tactically brilliant maneuver because it strikes at the heart of two names: God's name and our own name of Beloved. This question causes *us* to question—to grow suspicious, to doubt that God is really who God says he is. And if our spiritual enemy can incite a mistrust of God's nature, God's promises, and God's Word, then he can completely undermine our faith journey and destabilize our life's trajectory. Ultimately, if we don't trust God, we are unlikely to live sacrificially or passionately for God's name and God's Kingdom. We are unlikely to allow God to define much about us at all.

Consider this: *Did God really say . . . ?* can also mean:

- *Have God's boundaries for my life fallen in pleasant places?*
- *Is God withholding favor and blessing from me?*
- *Is God cruel?*
- *Is God all-powerful?*
- *Is God's Word true?*
- *Does God really have the "best" in store for me?*
- *Does God actually love me?*
- *Am I worthy of God's love?*
- *Am I enough?*
- *Does God actually see me? My dreams? My hopes?*

Like I said, *prudent*—because that one question contains countless other questions. *Did God really say . . . ?* can trigger all of the doubts and fears that lay dormant in our hearts: doubts about God's love, fears about his trustworthiness. All of it leading to a belief that we are unworthy and that God is unloving.

But there is a voice louder than the enemy's, a tactic stronger, wiser, and more farsighted than the garden serpent could ever hope to employ. Where Satan has a plot, God has a plan: Jesus.[7]

Jesus Christ, the Beloved Son of God, "f[ou]ght against and triumph[ed] over the evil powers of the world"[8] and in Jesus, God silences the voice of our enemy, the voice of rejection. In Jesus, we have a Savior and a Victor who died and rose again to forgive us, died and rose again to overcome the powers of evil and death in this world, and died and rose again "that we might," as author Rick Richardson suggests, "receive and believe the new name and fulfilled identity [God] calls us into."[9]

In fact, when we look to the baptism of Jesus, we find God speaking a new name and fulfilled identity over Jesus: "This is my beloved Son," the Father declares, "with whom I am well pleased" (Matthew 3:16-17, ESV).

In Jesus, this is also your inheritance, your fortune, and your promise—you are not unworthy, abandoned, or rejected.

In Jesus, you are declared *Beloved Daughter, Beloved Son*—with whom God is well pleased.

Oil, Wine, and Bandages

God called us Beloved from the beginning, and Jesus, God in the flesh, spoke Beloved over us again and again as he walked among us. The book of Luke records one of those moments. It's a story, actually, that Jesus told: about a man battered, a man bereft, a man broken by the sins of others. A man not unlike you and me. This man was attacked and robbed, then left for dead on the side of the road.

Many religious leaders walked past this man, blatantly choosing to neglect their hurting neighbor. And then—an enemy walked by. "A despised Samaritan"—a man whom the Jewish people would have dismissed and kept their distance from by virtue of his ethnicity and religion—saw the dying man and felt compassion for him.

Jesus describes in stunning detail what the good Samaritan's love looked like: "The Samaritan soothed [this man's] wounds with olive oil and wine and bandaged them. Then he put the man on his own donkey and took him to an inn, where he took care of him" (Luke 10:34, NLT).

Jesus paints a picture of a love that bears another's pain, a love that moves toward another, a love that nurses wounds, a love that brings the hurting person home, a love that provides, a love that heals, a love that deems the unlovable *worthy of love*. Though this is a story about how we ought to love our neighbors and our enemies, it is simultaneously a picture of the depth of God's love for us, even while we were still sinners, even while we were his enemies (Romans 5:8, 10).

This is not a *you are tolerated* kind of love.

Not an *I love you for your potential* kind of love.

Not a *strive and hustle* kind of love.

Not an *earn it if you're lucky* kind of love.

Not a *leave you in your ditch of despair* kind of love.

Not a *put you on a scale and measure you* kind of love.

Beloved, God's love for you in Christ is nothing short of all-consuming. His love is a love that triumphs over every abusive tactic, prudent or otherwise, of the enemy. God's love is anointing oil. His love is warm, soothing wine. His love is a bandage that binds. His love finds you, abandoned in your trauma and rejection, lifts you out, and brings you home, where your hungry, hurting soul can at last find its fill, can at last find its rest—in him.

Did God really say you are his Beloved?

Oh yes, my friend. He did.

This is your first name, your true name.

So breathe, little soul. Slow down, little heart. What are you striving for? What are you after? You already have God's approval and love. You are already known and accepted. You already have victory in Jesus. So return to your rest, for the Lord has been good to you.

Be loved, *Beloved.*

2

KNOWN

God Names Us Backward

For you created my inmost being;
   you knit me together in my mother's womb.
I praise you because I am fearfully and wonderfully made;
   your works are wonderful,
   I know that full well.
My frame was not hidden from you
   when I was made in the secret place,
   when I was woven together in the depths of the earth.
Your eyes saw my unformed body;
   all the days ordained for me were written in your book
   before one of them came to be.

PSALM 139:13-16

I don't know how life's longings and heartaches have touched you, shaped you, or made you, but I know one thing to be true: You were made in the secret place, and you are exceptionally loved and ferociously accepted by God who has been with you and who has carried your name with him since *before*.

You are, and have always been, entirely, deeply, and categorically *known*.

I AM UNCERTAIN IF MY FIRST CHILDHOOD MEMORY is an actual recollection or a memory born from my parent's retelling of it. Either way, the family legend goes like this:

My parents take me camping near a mountain close to our

home in Washington. It is the late spring of 1980, and I am just over two years old. In the middle of the night, I keep slipping out of my sleeping bag, unable to lay still, and my parents think I'm displaying some form of terrible-two defiance, until they discover the reason that I can't stay in my sleeping bag. It's the same reason they can't stay in their own sleeping bags.

The reason none of us can stay in our sleeping bags is because the ground is moving. And the reason the ground is moving is because the mountain is not a mountain; it is a volcano, and it is showing the very early signs of erupting. The way my (very southern) dad tells the story, "We hightailed it out of there, faster than green grass through a goose."

We were safe, but the eruption of Mount Saint Helens devastated Washington's ecology and economy. This was the Pacific Northwest's phoenix crumbling into ash and lava. Months later, our family moved from Washington to California, then eventually to Georgia, and from there to Oklahoma, the place where I first heard about this God-person named Jesus.

The day Jesus saved me still feels like a miracle, but I've always felt a tug of remorse that I didn't know God until I was almost a teenager. I feel that remorse, in part, because I missed out on Sunday school stories and games and cheesy 1980s evangelical kids' ministry fads, like "Psalty the Singing Songbook." But it's also because I just wish I knew Jesus my entire life.

Maybe this sounds greedy because so many people don't know Jesus until adulthood. I mean, I've had thirty years with him. What a gift! What a grace! But still, I have always wished I knew God in my childhood, always wondered if God's love intersected my life before I realized it. In fact, for the last year or so, I've been specifically asking God to show me something, anything, about his presence in my life before I knew him.

I recently walked through a spiritual practice related to childhood, inspired by C. S. Lewis's *Surprised by Joy*.[1] In this practice, a person is invited to spend some time considering and praying over his or her childhood and the ways God may have been reaching out or showing up. (This can be a triggering exercise for some who had a traumatic childhood, so it's important to make sure you feel safe to practice it.) When you feel ready, ask the Holy Spirit to illuminate moments from childhood where God was actively engaged with you. Do not allow condemnation or disapproval to speak to you. Just spend some time listening to God's loving voice as you consider the following experiences from childhood and/or adolescence:

- any meaningful experiences in nature (peace, awe, wonder, etc.)
- moments of connection or affirmation (with a parent or mentor)
- memories of being alone but not feeling alone
- experiences of being under the muse of creativity
- peak moments of joy in life events[2]

As I walked though this exercise, the Holy Spirit brought three specific childhood memories to mind.

- In California, at age five, I climbed to the top of my swing set and yelled up to the sky: "Hey you! Anybody there? Are you out there? Can you hear me?"

- In Georgia, at age eight, I played under a weeping willow tree in my backyard every morning before school, imagining that I was an elven princess, lost in the woods and frightened, waiting for someone to rescue me.

- In Oklahoma, at age eleven, I discovered a graveyard near my house, filled with centuries-old graves. I would pack a peanut butter and honey sandwich and have a picnic by my favorite one, a newer headstone among the ancients—the gravesite of a teenage boy whose stone was marked with this Shakespearian line:

> *When he shall die,*
> *Take him and cut him out in little stars,*
> *And he will make the face of heaven so fine*
> *That all the world will be in love with night*
> *And pay no attention to the garish sun.*[3]

I would eat my sandwich and sit on that grave and recite the epitaph aloud. I returned regularly to this gravestone because something about these words spoke to me (though I had to ask my mom what *garish* meant—"gaudy," she said). One question preoccupied me: Could someone's face actually shine so beautifully that it would cause the lovely sun to seem gaudy?

I wasn't sure, but I wanted to know someone like that.

The *Surprised by Joy* reflective exercise brought up a slew of mixed emotions. The wonderful truth it revealed is that in every state where we settled anew, I was always unknowingly searching for Someone outside of myself. Either that or that same Someone was searching for me.

But I also found myself feeling sort of vulnerable about these memories. Even though these aren't negative experiences, they seem oddly morbid. I mean, who sits at a grave by herself eating lunch? Who yells at an unknown being? Who pretends to be alone and afraid?

As I looked back on these instances in my childhood, I realized that instead of appreciating that God made me wonderfully curious, creative, and artistic, I have spent most of my adulthood looking back on my younger self—naming myself—as "that weird little girl" I used to be.

But now, as I am piecing these memories together with the Holy Spirit, I am starting to realize something healing and hopeful: God intentionally gave me a wildly alive imagination *so that* he could connect with me in my youth. My creativity and curiosity are beautiful, holy things, drawing me to God; they are part of how God has named me.

That said, there's another raw thing that the spiritual practice brought up. Almost directly after coming to Christ, I came up against sexual assault more than once. And over the years that followed, I have faced the tragic loss of loved ones, a personal battle with chronic illness, and mistakes and heartaches that accompany adolescence and adulthood. I have even sometimes wondered if my nearness to the tragedy of Mount Saint Helens shaped me, named me—as if, because I was there when it erupted, I was marked by its ash.

And yet, in the midst of all of these warring wonderings, I cannot shake this one thought: If I can find God active in my childhood, that means God has always been working, has always been with me, even in my most difficult days.

Of course, I believe these things to be true, *by faith*, by the confidence in what I cannot see. I understand that God is ever present, that God was always there, even in hardship. But selfishly, I want to know these truths through *encounter*.

I want to know that God was active in my childhood the way the Hebrew Scriptures talk about knowing—*yāḏaʾ*, knowing experientially and intimately. I want to experience for myself that David's audacious claims in Psalm 139 are true: "You knew me, Oh God, when I was made in the secret place. . . . Your eyes saw my unformed body" (author's paraphrase).

The Sacred Before

Psalm 139 is one of David's most personal and beautiful songs, full of intimate lines like, "You made all the delicate, inner parts of my body and knit me together in my mother's womb. Thank you for making me so wonderfully complex! Your workmanship is marvelous—how well I know it" (NLT). *The Message* Bible translation says it like this: "I thank you, High God—you're breathtaking! Body and soul, I am marvelously made!"

In years past, I have read this psalm as a confidence booster. When I was feeling insecure or in a self-rejection place, I'd read Psalm 139 aloud and remind myself that God has made me fearfully and wonderfully, in his image. I'd concentrate on how deliberate and poetic my very existence is. I've prayed this prayer as a prophetic word over others who were questioning their self-esteem or worth. Psalm 139 gives us emotional strength; God has designed us with love, artistry, and intentionality.

But I've been rereading Psalm 139, especially in view of those childhood memories. And this time through, my soul has been drawn to one word in particular, a word that David uses sparingly but forcefully: *before*.

> *Before* a word is on my tongue
>   you, LORD, know it completely.
> You hem me in behind and *before* . . .
> Your eyes saw my unformed body;
>   all the days ordained for me were written in your book
>   *before* one of them came to be.
> PSALM 139:4-5, 16, EMPHASIS ADDED

David declares with awe that God saw, God loved, God knew, God moved, God worked, God called, God protected, God planned, God ordained *before*. Before can mean "at the forefront of," as in, "you hem me in behind and before." It can also mean "prior to." But before can also mean the sacred before—that sheltered, secret place of God's heart and God's dreams, where everything that would exist first began to exist.

When you think of your own existence, do you wonder what God was up to, regarding you—before you came into being? Was he creatively dreaming about your hair type and skin color and eye color and life's narrative? Were you born in a flash of holy brilliance or over a long period in the timeless expanse of God's omnipresence? Did God know your name even then?

The Bible answers with a resounding *yes!* to all of these questions. God knew you, formed you, watched you before even one day of your life came to pass. In the sacred before, God was already longing to lead you along the path of everlasting life. Though your childhood may have felt void of his presence, it wasn't. He was there, loving you into being all along.

Surprised by a Name

As God would have it, the same week I practice the *Surprised by Joy* spiritual exercise and start working through these issues regarding my childhood, I am entering my final session of spiritual direction. After almost four years, my time with my spiritual director is ending.

To be frank with you, I began meeting with my spiritual director as a last resort. I was in deep grief, lament, heartache, and pain and wasn't sure if I believed God existed. And if God existed, I wasn't sure if I cared. But with my spiritual director's gracious help and the Holy Spirit's power, I have felt God's presence again, and my faith has exploded into a deeper, realer faith than before. It has been with her that I've been given graceful permission to doubt, to question, and to wonder. I have experienced God's wholeness and love through spiritual direction, and I will be eternally grateful. (I highly recommend finding a spiritual director if you need that kind of space.)

The COVID-19 pandemic has forced us to shift to meeting online, and so for this last session together, we're meeting over computer screens instead of in person. I wonder what Saint Ignatius would think of us meeting over technology and the internet as we use his Examen to reflect on our time together. Still, we give our four years a name—*grace*.

When our session wraps up, my director tells me this, "Aubrey, there is an image and a word that God has given me for you. It's something, I believe, that is meant to describe you. Let me put it on the screen."

She shares a picture of a white flower with a sunshine-yellow center, springing up from a pile of charcoal gray ash. "This is an avalanche lily. It's a flower that only grows in dead places."

The metaphor is obvious, life springing from death, beauty sprouting from debris. "You have done the dangerous work of searching for God when you thought you would never find him again," she said. "And you have an explosive amount of image-bearing in you. You are an avalanche lily, my friend, coming to life after death."

I'm wiping away a few tears, touched by this moment. But my spiritual director is not finished speaking. "I'm not sure why," she continues, "but for some reason, I sensed that God wanted me to show you a particular avalanche lily—one that grows in a specific area of the country."

With this, she pulls up a second image of a lily. It's similar to the first, though this one is not growing from ash. It's growing from magma.

"This is the image I felt the Holy Spirit wanting me to show you. It's an avalanche lily. This one grows on Mount Saint Helens."

I am silent, stunned. Tears erupt, and I am nearly sobbing.

She doesn't understand the new force of my emotions, and, assuming it's just the word picture of the lily that has moved me, she goes on: "You might be too young to remember this, but Mount Saint Helens erupted about forty years ago. The people of Washington never thought the site would be restored, but now it contains more lush life than it had before the eruption."

I interrupt her train of thought to ask for clarification, just in case I am imagining this moment. "I'm sorry. Did you say God wanted you to show me this specific avalanche lily? Or did you choose this because *you* like this one?"

"I know it's weird," she replies, "but God gave me this specific image and this particular location to show you. I think he wants you to know that beauty will rise from . . ."

I cut her off with even more sobbing, wiping my eyes and grabbing Kleenex to blow my nose. "It's not that. I know what it is. I was there when it started to erupt. I was camping with my parents. We had to evacuate. It's this whole family legend."

I'm trying to make sense of what has just happened, and I experience the realization at the same time I try to explain it. "I've been praying for a while now that God would show me that he was there in my childhood. I think this is my answer. God is telling me he was there—and is showing me through this image he gave you."

"What?" she asks in disbelief. Then she starts to tear up, and soon we're both a mess of tears and snot and wonder.

We end our time together in awe and worship because what else can we do after such a holy moment? Who but God could orchestrate such a narrative? Who are we mortals that God is mindful of us? Whose face could shine so brightly that it would cause the sun to seem garish?

Only Jesus.

After our session, I close my computer and grab my journal to write a prayer based on Psalm 139:

I can never escape from your Spirit! I can never get
away from your presence! If I go up to a swing set, you
are there. If I walk through willow tree branches in the
morning, even there your hand will guide me, your
strength will support me. If I sit and have lunch by a
graveside, you are there. And Lord, even if I camp near
a volcano when it erupts, you are there. I praise you
because you watched me before I was born. Your eyes
have seen me my entire life. How precious to me are your
thoughts about me, O God. You have always been and
will always be with me. Such knowledge is too wonderful
for me, too great for me to understand. I praise you!

A few days later, a package arrives in the mail. There's a card
from my spiritual director that says, "God has been with you since
before you were born," and the box contains a framed picture of
the avalanche lily from Mount Saint Helens. She has included
the caption from the original photo, which reads: "Life returns
to Mount St. Helens. Avalanche lilies (Erythronium montanum)
growing through blast deposits from May 18 eruption, 1980."

While working on this book, I've asked God for a name—a
name that only God would be able to speak over me, a name that
would pierce through the secret places of my soul's longing with
healing and offer answers. I've simultaneously been asking him to
reveal his presence in my childhood. God was silent on both fronts
for what seemed like a long time.

To be totally honest with you, I wanted a "name" from God so
you would know that what I'm talking about in this book is real. I
wanted to be able to tell you that I have a powerful, personal name
from God—and he wants to name you too! Naming and renaming is a
massive part of the Holy Spirit's ministry, and I've longed to experience
it. But more than any of that, my desire for a "name" goes back to my

desire to know God. I want to know that God knows me the way no one else can know me—because *to be known is to be intimately loved.* And I want to know God's expansive love more and more.

Even as I asked for a name, I expected God to name me by something I do: "Preacher Girl" or "Writer" or something like that. Instead, as only God can, he names me immeasurably beyond what I could ask or imagine. God has named me from being, not doing. Just as he has likely named you. And he has named me from the place of a first memory, from the ethos inside of me and my family. God has brought my entire life's longings together in the most explosive way possible—with more eruptive healing than my heart can hold at once.

My name is Avalanche Lily, and God has known me since the sacred before.

———— ◆ ————

Do I believe Mount Saint Helens erupted just so that forty years later I would know my name? Of course not. God does not cause annihilation or evil. But I do believe something else—something new.

Sometimes God names us backward to show us that he has been there our entire lives. Though we might be touched by lava, ash, and eruption, destruction is not the final word for us. Devastation is never the first or the last name spoken over us.

I don't know how life's longings and heartaches have touched you, shaped you, or made you, but I know one thing to be true: You were made in the secret place, and you are exceptionally loved and ferociously accepted by God who has been with you and who has carried your name with him since *before.*

You are, and have always been, entirely, deeply, and categorically *known.*

3

NEEDY

Deeply Embedded Names

[God] blessed them and called them "human."

GENESIS 5:2, NLT

Part of being human means that we require having our needs met by Someone outside of us. In fact, we are most human in our need for God. To deny that is to deny our authentic humanity.

I guess what I am saying is this: Fine, I'm needy. So are you. We're human, after all. Beautifully needy humans.

"AUBREY, AUBREY, YES OF COURSE! Yes, brilliant! Your name is Aubrey! Did your mother name you after a character in a book?"

Cartoon cherubs and hearts are floating around Nigel's head as he speaks to me. I've been waiting patiently in line to talk to this British actor, who is visiting our college for the day, but his accent and general English demeanor is so adorably distracting that I can barely answer his question. "Yes!" I squeak out, blushing a little. "How'd you know?"

I'm an unabashed Anglophile. My roommate has a British professor whose office we call after hours just to hear the Queen's English on his voice-mail message: "Well, blimey and 'ello mates!

You've reached Professor Charleston's office. I'm down at the pub, wearing trainers and a jumper, eating fish and chips, and listening to a right-proper Beatles cover band. Leave a message, or you're mental! Cheers!" (It didn't really say that.) And that summer, I had backpacked my way across Great Britain.

All that to say, I'm feeling especially girlish right now as I chat with this REAL! LIVE! FAMOUS! BRIT! standing in front of me. I'm trying to act effortless, nonchalant, but the moment anyone tries for nonchalance, its purpose is defeated. Make no mistake, I intentionally mention my love of Guinness and the Globe Theatre to try to impress him.

Nigel (we're on a first-name basis in my mind) spoke to the entire college this morning, and now our college acting troupe is getting access—exclusive access—to him.

"Aubrey! Aubrey! What a name!" he declares dramatically. "You know what you must do, don't you?"

I don't know, but please tell me, I beg silently, willing myself to remember his every syllable.

"If you're going to be alive, if you want to be fully human, then you must lift your name from the page! Lift it! Lift it! Lift it!" He gesticulates theatrically while making this declaration.

"Yes, I understand. I will," I say, nodding seriously.

A friend grabs me by the elbow as we walk away together. "Did you have any idea what he was saying?"

"Not a clue," I confess, and we break out into fits of giggles.

And then, a few seconds later, an old, involuntary refrain rises in me: *You're so needy*.

I push it down, ignoring it.

Later, our little drama group sits cross-legged in a circle on the hardwood floor of our black-box theater. All of us are awestruck as Nigel tells us about a new television pilot he's working on. He's playing a young pastor who has left the ministry but is still a practicing Christian and is now navigating the world of dating. "It is a comedy," he tells us. (Looking back now, it sounds depressing. No wonder it never got picked up.)

"The scriptwriters and television execs often ask for my advice about this character. Because"—Nigel inhales dramatically, then exhales as he speaks—"I . . . am . . . a . . . Christian."

This isn't a shock to any of us; we're at an evangelical Christian college, after all. But it's clearly meant to be a bombshell. So we all sort of gasp, knowing we're supposed to. Then Nigel says something that, two decades later, I still think about.

"They ask me how this Christian character would behave out in the real world. If this character's motivation is to live a God-fearing life, what would he actually do? Would he lie? Would he steal? Would he drink and do drugs? Would he date several women at once? Would he have sex with any of them?"

"Here is what I tell them," he continues. "This bloke is not that different from anyone else. He would do all the things someone who isn't a Christian would do. The only difference is . . . he would feel guilty afterward."

I look around the circle, and some of my theater friends are nodding in agreement or mumbling "Mmm" under their breath, deeply impressed by this profound understanding of his character. He's about to move on to another point when I interrupt, "Wait! I have something to say!"

To be clear: I do this in my mind. I don't actually say anything aloud because I'm already fantasizing about marrying him and birthing his British babies, and I don't want to jinx my future plans.

But I am, genuinely, more than a little dismayed that my future babies' daddy doesn't bring a bit more theological acumen to our burgeoning relationship. (Perhaps I should have known then that

I'd marry a pastor and also become a pastor myself in the future.) What I want to say is, "What the what?! The only difference between a Christian and a non-Christian is *guilt*?"

I start to work up the nerve to raise my hand in real life, to beg to differ and offer another point of view. I'm kind of thrilled, actually, to banter with Nigel the Brit. But I'm jolted again by that familiar refrain: *You are so needy. You just want attention.*

I stop myself from saying anything.

Deeply Embedded Names

Once, I accidentally left a bag of garbage in the trunk of my car overnight, and the next morning when I went to throw it in the bin, I found dozens of squirming maggots embedded in the upholstery of my trunk. I spent hours using a pair of tweezers to tediously remove each maggot one by one, all while trying my best not to vomit.

That is what the name Needy did. That name planted itself firmly in the fabric of my psyche after a horrific incident, my second experience of sexual assault, the second occurrence of blaming myself because "I was needy; I wanted attention."

Our words matter—and also, they have matter. The names we speak over ourselves are weighty. They teach others how to think about us; they train us how to think about ourselves. They reveal who we believe we really are in the world and in God's eyes. They expose our passions and loves but also our deep-seated wounds, fears, and inadequacies. As the poet Maya Angelou said,

> Words are things. You must be careful, careful about
> calling people out of their names, using racial pejoratives
> and sexual pejoratives and all that ignorance. Don't do
> that. Someday we'll be able to measure the power of
> words. I think they are things. I think they get on the

walls. They get in your wallpaper. They get in your rugs, in your upholstery and your clothes, and finally, into you.[1]

This is one of the larger, unspoken wounds festering inside many of us. Though each of us is named by God, we unknowingly allow false names to come for a visit, get comfortable, and dig down deep into our soul's upholstery. That's what I did with the name Needy. The fact that for many years I labeled myself this belittling thing—like it was no big deal, like it was my zip code or Wi-Fi password—well, it still shakes me even now when I think about it.

But there is actually a gift in the strange moment with Nigel in the theater. As Needy whispers itself over me again, I begin to grasp a thread of what "Lift your name from the page" means, though it's probably not what Nigel the Brit intends:

We all have names upon names that need to be lifted, removed, eradicated from the pages of our lives, from the fabric of our souls, before healing and human flourishing can be written there.

Later that evening, I sit in the theater alone in the dark, silently pleading with God to release me, or at least speak a better word over me. *God, please erase the name Needy from my page. Replace it with another name, any other name.*

Many years later, God does. But not even close to the way I expect.

Name Reconstruction

Years after that evening in the theater, I sit in a hospital bed with a brand-new name: Mom. I hold my firstborn son, the first of three humans whom I will help make and name and bring into the world over the next decade. Tenderly, I examine each soft, little toe and each sweet, tiny finger, in awe of his miraculous existence.

Simply because my son exists, I adore him. I am fiercely for him in a way that I have never been for anyone else in my life. I notice the way his head smells like maple syrup, how soft and supple his skin is. I notice that his cries cause me to forget that anything else in the world exists.

There is something else I notice as well.

He is so desperately needy, so utterly dependent on me. His entire survival is contingent on me. But this neediness, this limitedness, this dependence, is so remarkable, so magical, so soft, so sweet and vulnerable, it makes my heart ache.

As I hold my son, I begin to hear the answer to my prayer in that theater so long ago. I begin to understand that to "lift the name Needy from the pages of my life" is not to erase it. It is to allow God to reconstruct my understanding of it.

I may have named myself Needy all those years ago. Named, from the part of myself that was wounded deeply by the sins of others. But in this hospital bed, the love of God supernaturally intersects the broken way I name myself. It is here where I discover that God doesn't always erase our false names.

Sometimes God meets our false names with such powerful redemption that they become the very place of our renewal.

I know I am healed from Needy, not because I no longer think of myself as needy but because when I hold my newborn babies for the first time, I begin to marvel at something anew. To be needy is actually a part of being human.

When Adam and Eve sinned, first beginning to know good and evil, perhaps it wasn't the knowledge itself that was the problem. Maybe, just maybe, it's that Adam and Eve took it upon themselves, as John F. Kilner suggests, the "responsibility for distinguishing good and evil."[2] Maybe just maybe, in their wanting to be like God, they tried to make themselves autonomous from God.[3] They decided they were no longer needy for God.

Genesis 5:2 says that God blessed us and called us "humans." And part of being human means that we require having our needs met by Someone outside of us. In fact, we are most human in our need for God. To deny that is to deny our authentic humanity.

I guess what I am saying to Mr. British Actor, to myself, and to you is this: Fine, I'm needy. So are you. We're human, after all. Beautifully needy humans.

———◆———

If there's a broken name deeply embedded in your soul's fabric, you have options. You can try pushing it down, but that only works for a few years. The name will pop up at the most inopportune moments. You can also try digging it out like I did with the maggots in my car's trunk, but that gets ugly and gross. A better option is to invite the Spirit of God to tend to your false name.

In so doing, you'll find that your name shares space with redemption.

4

UNVEILED

Ooze and Bones

All of us who have had that veil removed can see and reflect
the glory of the Lord. And the Lord—who is the Spirit—
makes us more and more like him as we are changed into
his glorious image.

2 CORINTHIANS 3:18, NLT

When we put our trust in Christ, we who were once Veiled have been renamed; we are Unveiled in Jesus, which means we are becoming more and more like Jesus as we participate in life with his Spirit.

THERE IS A CORNER IN MY READING ROOM where I store my issues, the things I often try to hide from God and others.

If I find that I'm craving esteem or recognition in an unhealthy way, and if, in that craving, my ego has started maniacally planning all the ways I can get it, I'll stop and say, "Oh hey! There's that issue again. I know this one well. This is the part of me that loves approval and power. It doesn't belong here in my head or in my heart or even in my hands. It fits better over here, in my corner."

Then I will physically walk over to the reading-room corner and imagine myself placing that particular issue there for safekeeping.

Let's say I'm tempted to spend more money than I have because there's some new product that promises to make me feel momentarily happy and light. That's when I go, "Oof! There it is again, my old pal materialism. This is the part of me that doesn't trust God to fulfill me or provide for me. This is the hungry part that wants and wants and wants. It belongs right here, in the reading-room corner."

When I catch myself fantasizing about running away from my responsibilities because they feel like too much? "Ugh! There's that issue again, the one where I feel unseen and overwhelmed. Yikes. It keeps trying to get close to me, but it actually fits perfectly in the corner. I'm going to gently place it there again."

Mind you, the reading-room corner is not a time-out corner; it's not a dunce-cap corner. It's not a place to punish my issues or hide them. The reading-room corner is where God and I have agreed that I will surrender my struggles to him, where I will be as vulnerable as I can with him, so that he can take care of my issues, so that I don't keep managing and pretending.

Sometimes, ceremoniously, I'll even add a sentiment of gratitude when placing my issue down, "Thank you, God, for this issue, because it keeps me returning to you. It reminds me that you are God and I am not, and I desperately need you to transform me."

I used to approach my issues with derision, with a kind of *Aubrey, you know better than this, you dummy! Why are you struggling with this again?* energy. But I've discovered it's much more advantageous to move toward my issues the same way I'd approach a child lost at the grocery store. "Can I help you, hon?" I ask, gently, "Is there some better place you need to be? Let's find the one who takes care of you. Let me take you there."

And if I am delicate, carefully offering my hand to my issues, I find that they see me as an ally and will walk with me, amiably, to their proper place in the reading-room corner.

I actually do this, again and again and again, because I believe a somewhat fantastical notion that this corner of my home is a holy space, that spiritual transformation occurs here, and that something supernatural takes place inside of me when I name things rightly and relinquish them to God.

I even believe that a little eternal flame, a burning bush, blazes there in my reading-room corner, ever welcoming and warm, ever ready for my soul's surrender.

———————

I have a squad of best friends, the really good kind. One is the kind of woman who you can tell about your Reading-Room Issue Corner and she gets it because she is self-aware about her own issues and because she also believes in sacred spaces among ordinary things.

That said, she is also the kind of friend who, when she notices that you've been in your head too long about your issues—if you're spending too much time wading near the bottom of your sad pool of self-reflection—will belly flop into the water just to make you laugh.

She's the friend who can woo you out of your emotional death spiral with a perfectly timed, inappropriate joke. She will bake you homemade cookies that spell out *You can do hard things!* (I don't bake anything. She bakes the alphabet.)

What I mean, ultimately, is that she's the kind of friend who when you think of her, you think, *Yup, that's my person.*

This year, my best friend, my person, was diagnosed with an aggressive form of breast cancer.

This year, I have spent many sleepless nights pleading for her life.

This year, I have fasted and prayed and slayed cancer demons on her behalf.

This year, our squad has worn camo on Wednesdays because Wednesday is chemo day and that means Wednesday has become #WarriorWednesday.

This year, my friend and her husband and their three young sons have bravely endured the worst kind of nightmare, and it has all felt like more than any corner in any reading room in the world can hold.

But I know that's not true because nothing is greater than what God can hold.

So when I bring all of my issues about my best friend to that corner, I say: "Okay, God, this right here, this thing I'm surrendering to you, it's a tender thing. This is the part of me that is afraid. This is also the part of me that is really angry at you. It's the part that isn't sure that you are bigger than cancer. I know you are, but what if you decide not to be this time? So I am choosing to say thank you and choosing to trust you because she is my person and I need you to show up here. God, you have to show up here."

When faced with the worst life has to offer, what can we do but keep showing up to these sacred corners with our whole and contradictory selves in tow? These corners are gifts of grace, after all. And so often, grace is all we have to go on.

Cocoon Ooze and Rattling Bones

In the apostle Paul's second letter to the Corinthian church, a hurting church (who, by the way, often seem a little peeved at Paul; half of Paul's subtext to them sounds like, "Dudes, you need to calm down."), he reminds this messy group of Christ followers about something profound. Paul tells them this: "We all, who with unveiled faces contemplate the Lord's glory, are being transformed into his image with ever-increasing glory, which comes from the Lord, who is the Spirit" (2 Corinthians 3:18).

What Paul means is that "the veil," that thing that used to blind us from *seeing* God's glory and keep us from *reflecting* God's glory, has been removed from the faces of those who follow Jesus. When we put our trust in Christ, we who were once Veiled have been renamed; we are Unveiled in Jesus, which means we are becoming more and more like him as we participate in life with his Spirit.

This is a beautiful paradox of our spiritual formation. We are unveiled immediately through our faith in Christ, *and* we are ever-increasingly unveiled as we continue following him throughout our lives.

Another way of saying this is that you and I are in the process of becoming who we already are. You and I are being transformed into who God has already declared us to be. We are unveiled in order to become more like Jesus.

The term Paul uses here in 2 Corinthians 3:18 for "being transformed," is *metamorfoō*, where we get the word *metamorphosis*. And for a long time I thought the process of spiritual metamorphosis was something akin to a children's story. You know, as if "Metamorphosis" is a chubby and clumsy caterpillar who, one day, decides to knit a cozy little sleeping bag for himself. He crawls inside, falls asleep, has some very sweet dreams, and then emerges, albeit a bit inelegantly, and surprise! Now he has colorful wings and a little golden crown on his head. *What a loveable little knucklehead, that Metamorphosis!*

But a caterpillar's *actual* metamorphosis is much closer to a sci-fi or horror movie. *Scientific American* teaches us that "the caterpillar digests itself, releasing enzymes to dissolve all of its tissues. If you were to cut open a cocoon or chrysalis at just the right time, caterpillar soup would ooze out."[1]

Within the tight confines of its cocoon, the creature disintegrates, and yet somehow, while reduced to what is essentially little more than an "amorphous mess"[2]—a near-nothingness—some of its cells miraculously survive. From there, a butterfly's chrysalis forms. The once-caterpillar is reborn, transformed.

Our spiritual metamorphosis is a lot like *that*. In fact, later in his letter to the Corinthians, Paul explains that transformation into Christlikeness occurs through our cocoon seasons. "Through suffering," writes the apostle, "our bodies continue to share in the death of Jesus so that the life of Jesus may also be seen in our bodies" (2 Corinthians 4:10, NLT).

In other words, suffering leads to a greater unveiling of Jesus' image in us. That sounds discouraging certainly, but what Paul is telling this hurting, persecuted, suffering church—and reminding us of as well—is that in our painful seasons, in our heartache and grief, we are pressed but not completely crushed. We may get knocked down, but we are never totally destroyed.

Through all of our issues, as we stay surrendered to and focused on Jesus, we continually transform and grow more luminous.[3] This is the kind of miracle that only a loving, powerful God could execute; we emerge from life's cocoon seasons re-created into greater Christlikeness.

The apostle Paul lets us in on a secret about our unveiling. This whole journey of spiritual metamorphosis comes from the Spirit of God (2 Corinthians 3:18). That means we are never alone in our suffering and also that our pain is not purposeless; the Lord's Spirit always transforms gall into glory.

In fact, there's an old story about the Holy Spirit that Paul indirectly refers to elsewhere in 2 Corinthians (3:3). It's the story of the prophet Ezekiel, whom God gave a vision, a prophetic word about a land of scattered dry bones, a valley of death.

"See those dead bones, Ezekiel?" God said to the prophet, "I want you to do something powerful and authoritative. I want you to declare and command newness and transformation over these bones. I want you to speak life into those lifeless bodies by saying, 'Dry bones, listen up! You will live again!'" (Ezekiel 37:4-6, author's paraphrase).

Ezekiel obeyed and watched as these brittle bones morphed from near-nothingness to newfound life.

Sometimes the space between who we are and who we want to be is wide. The chasm between where we are now and where we hope to land in the future seems vast and daunting. Sometimes our fears come a lot closer to home than we are prepared for, and sometimes life feels dry. The promise of 2 Corinthians 3:18 is that in Jesus, brittle seasons become unveiling seasons, bursting with glory, breath, and new life.

———

My best friend's hair has fallen out. Her tumor has grown. Her cancer has spread. Through it all, she is fighting and resting, wrestling and surrendering. She is becoming who she already is—gloriously unveiled in Christ.

All of it—her cancer, my ongoing issues, and your cocoon moments—are invitations into greater transformation and deeper intimacy with God's grace. I'll say it again: So often, grace is all we have—all we *need*—to go on.

And so we go on, claiming the promises that are ours in Christ.

In Jesus—

Reading-room corners become altars.

Dry bones start to rattle.

Disintegration makes way for gossamer wings.

5

WHOLE

Defined by Victory

God created human beings in his own image.
In the image of God he created them;
male and female he created them.

GENESIS 1:27, NLT

You get to decide when you are ready to shake off the dust
of rejection, shame, and insecurity and walk away.

You get to decide when you are ready to move toward
Jesus and ask him to make you whole.

I WAS SEXUALLY ASSAULTED on a school bus at age thirteen and four years later by an employer at an after-school job. I have written about these experiences elsewhere,[1] but it is never my favorite thing to do, to revisit those moments when I felt like a nameless object, used for someone else's consumption.

My reluctance is not so much about the distressing experiences themselves. I have been through a beautiful journey of healing in Christ, and I am grateful for every opportunity I get to share the powerful story of how God stepped in to heal me, removing my shame and pain. Because of God's love, my wounds are not my identity. I will keep on sharing that until I die.

It's just that I am deeply uninterested in my trauma becoming the defining narrative of my life.

Matthew, Mark, and Luke's Gospels each include a story about a woman known only as "a woman having an issue of blood" (Luke 8:43, ASV; see also Matthew 9:20; Mark 5:25). At the beginning of the story, she is defined as no more than her past: She'd bled for twelve years straight, chronically tormented by her illness, isolated from her community because of it.

I don't want my name to become "the woman with the issue of her trauma."

But here's the thing: That "woman having an issue of blood" *didn't stay defined by that.* She chose to move toward Jesus, and he changed her name—and her story.

The bleeding woman took a massive risk one day and joined the throng of people who were following this extraordinary guy. When she finally drew close enough to see him, still separated by the clamoring crowd, she stretched her entire self toward Jesus. All her hope, all her wounds, all her doubt, all her heartache, and all her trembling vulnerability grasped like a drowning person reaches for life, and she touched the hem of his clothes. Barely a brush of contact, but that connection with Jesus erased the thing that had defined her for so long. Suddenly, in an instant, she was whole.

Just a _____

A little while after his encounter with the bleeding woman, the Son of God returned to his hometown to continue his ministry among family and friends. And when I say "ministry," I mean performing miracles, healing people, overcoming evil, teaching with power, and transforming lives. Jesus was literally personifying the Kingdom of God.

Yet even though this is *Jesus,* and even though he's doing all these glory-of-God-worthy things, his friends and neighbors don't take him seriously. "He's just the carpenter's son," they say dismissively (Matthew 13:55, NLT). *We knew him when he was little. We know his family. He's nothing special.*

I love that this story is in Scripture because we all have some "He's *just* a carpenter" refrain on repeat: places where our pasts or our brokenness or our sense of notenoughness define us. While "carpenter" may not be your exact kryptonite, maybe your "He's/She's just a _____" line of thinking goes something like this—

- *I'm just a stay-at-home parent—what do I have to offer the world?*
- *I'm just a fake.*
- *I'm just a mess.*
- *I'm just too angry/bossy/controlling.*
- *I'm just an idiot.*
- *I'm just unoriginal; everyone has already done that before or done it better than I could.*
- *I'm just too weak.*
- *I'm just too sensitive, too emotional.*
- *I'm just a terrible sinner.*
- *I'm just alone.*
- *I'm just too old or too young.*
- *I'm just too fat. (This one really has nothing to do with anything, but it seems to come up for all of us, so I thought I'd add it here for good measure.[2])*
- *I'm just unworthy.*
- *I'm just afraid of what others will think.*

Or, maybe your "I'm just a _____" beliefs are more along the lines of something like this:

- *Everyone will realize I have no idea what I'm doing.*
- *I didn't go to college or get a Bible degree, so I have nothing important to say.*
- *I'm broken, a failure.*
- *I'm disqualified.*
- *My best years are behind me.*
- *I'm damaged goods.*
- *I'm too traumatized.*

Perhaps your "I'm just a _____ statement" looks a bit like a question: *Who do you think you are?* Who do you think you are to . . . see your dreams come true, lead in greater capacity, have your words heard and mean something, speak with authority, believe God has good plans for you?

This list could get endless, so I'll stop before we're all thoroughly dejected. The point is, it gets noisy up in there in our insecurity, doesn't it? We all have a lot of definitions rattling around in our heads. It can feel defeating.

But we can learn a little something from Jesus in this "prophet in his own hometown without honor" moment. Because Jesus fully embraced his identity as God's beloved Son, everything he did was *from* a position of approval, not *for* it. So this hometown rejection didn't shake him. The definitions of his past didn't stick to him.

Jesus shook the dust off his feet and walked away from those who misnamed him.

———•———

If you have embarked on any kind of healing journey—because of grief, trauma, chronic pain, severe illness, rejection, or insecurity of some kind—you know that there are well-meaning advocates out there who will tell you things like, "You are not a victim. You are a victor."

I agree with that statement, wholeheartedly. I am that well-meaning advocate.

However.

True healing for anyone who has borne the pain of another person's depravity in their bodies; true empowerment for anyone who has carried sin, not from within but sin inflicted from without; true wholeness for anyone working through chronic issues; true health for anyone working their namedness struggles—demands that *that person* decides when he or she is ready to claim the victory that is theirs in Christ.

You get to decide when you are ready to shake off the dust of rejection, shame, and insecurity and walk away.

You get to decide when you are ready to move toward Jesus and ask him to make you whole.

Victory in Christ is yours for the taking.

Made Whole

There's another part of the woman with an issue of blood's story that I want to share with you. It's actually my favorite part.

After healing power went out from him, Jesus longed to find the person who touched him. So he combed through the unyielding crowd, ignoring his friends who tried to stop him. Jesus looked and looked and looked until the woman realized that she could not remain unfound any longer. Ever so cautiously, she came near, falling at Jesus' feet, afraid of the repercussions of her boldness.

But right there, right in front of her watching hometown, right in front of the community who had labeled her Unclean and

Outcast for over a decade, Jesus spoke a blessing and new name over her:

"Daughter," he declared, "Your faith has healed you. Go in peace."

No longer "a woman having an issue of blood." Defined by isolation. Defined by shame.

Instead, "Daughter." Defined by relationship. Defined by belonging. Defined by wholeness.

This is the real reason why I don't want the telling thing about me to be "the woman who was twice assaulted." Partly because others have far more painful journeys than mine. And partly because I get exhausted, emotionally, from reliving the memories.

But mostly, because like the woman with the issue of blood, I am not defined by my pain anymore. I have encountered Jesus. When I couldn't muscle the wherewithal to be brave, he looked for me. He found me. And he called me Daughter.

And then?

I rose, covered in and overcome by his victory. I became whole.

A miniscule amount of faith is all it takes to grasp the hem of Jesus' endless power and inexhaustible possibility. You, friend, are invited to reach out and rise up.

6

(RE)NAMED

God Names Us Forward

What are mere mortals that you should think about them,
   human beings that you should care for them?
Yet you made them only a little lower than God
   and crowned them with glory and honor.

PSALM 8:4-5, NLT

In place of the damaging names you have carried, the Holy Spirit, as in the ancient days, wants to speak a new name—a forward name and a freeing name—over you.

You are Renamed.

Don't listen to any other names than the ones God calls you.

"THE NAME I WAS GIVEN WAS 'PIGGY.'"

I'm at a small gathering of ministry and marketplace leaders, a weeklong training of sorts. A few hours into our third day together, the speaker suddenly interrupts his own train of thought. He removes his reading glasses, tucks them mindlessly into his shirt collar, and says, "I'm sensing from the Holy Spirit that we are supposed to stop what we're doing and pray right now, specifically for someone who needs emotional healing."

The small classroom is silent as he looks around, an expectant question mark on his face. Just as the moment threatens to tiptoe into awkwardness, a woman near the back of the small auditorium sheepishly raises her hand, tears already forming in her eyes. "It's me. You're supposed to pray for me. I *need* prayer today."

She consents to us gathering around her. Our speaker walks over to stand near her, while a few of us get up from our seats to place our hands on her shoulders. The rest reach hands out toward her. All of us, the body of Christ, enfolding her.

Our speaker begins the time of prayer, but then pauses as if he is listening to something. After a slight interval, he says this, "Jesus is telling me there is a name you've had since childhood, a nickname that was written on a memorable object that has caused you a lot of pain. You don't have to tell us what it was. But does that make sense to you?"

She nods, tears trickling down her cheeks. "Yes, I know what the name is. I know what the object is."

"Jesus is saying he wants to root out that name from your soul and replace it with *his* name for you. Are you ready for that?"

"Definitely," she replies with a small chuckle of relief through her tears.

He goes on, "Jesus wants you to know that you are beautiful. This is his name for you—My Beautiful One."

At the sound of that name, her tears become an uncontainable gush of emotion because what none of us know then—what she will tell us later—is this:

The name I was given was "Piggy." It was my nickname growing up. When I was twelve years old, it was written on my birthday cake. I have carried an underlying shame about my appearance for over thirty years because of it. And today, even before he asked if anyone needed prayer, my shame was speaking loudly. When he spoke those specific words, I knew they were from God. If they weren't, this man we barely know would not have said those things in a room full of men and women. Those are the exact words I have been longing to hear for nearly three decades. Only God knew that.[1]

I have thought about that day so often over the years because it helped me realize two things: (1) sharing Jesus with other people is often about creating space for them to be known, fully known—no masks, no pretenses—and allowing them to encounter God's healing love; and (2) names matter deeply to God. God loves to erase heartrending names from our pasts so that he can name us forward, so that he can move us into the dignity and destiny he has for us.[2]

Ugandan theologian Emmanuel M. Katongole explains that for many cultures, "the naming of a baby is never a private or family matter; it is a social event, and the name is understood not simply as personal tag, chosen because it is 'cute,' but as the embodiment of social memory and a form of practical wisdom."[3]

God is aware that our names, whether true or false, can become self-fulfilling prophecies with the power to dictate the way we live.[4] So when he gives his children new names, God isn't being cute.

When God renames, he re-creates.

God's (Re)Naming Ministry

The psalmist declares, "What are mere mortals that you should think about them, human beings that you should care for them? Yet you made them only a little lower than God and crowned them with glory and honor" (Psalm 8:4-5, NLT).

Who are we, that God should be mindful of our names? And yet our loving, powerful, all-knowing God is always singing out who we are now and declaring who we will one day become.

You, *beloved of God*, have been named honorably by God. He is calling you out of your false names and old names into the new, redemptive names he has for you. How do we know he does this? Because this is what God has always done.

Abraham and Sarah

> When Abram was ninety-nine years old, the LORD appeared to him and said, "I am God Almighty; walk before me faithfully and be blameless. Then I will make my covenant between me and you and will greatly increase your numbers."
>
> Abram fell facedown, and God said to him, "As for me, this is my covenant with you: You will be the father of many nations. No longer will you be called Abram; your name will be Abraham, for I have made you a father of many nations. I will make you very fruitful; I will make nations of you, and kings will come from you. I will establish my covenant as an everlasting covenant between me and you and your descendants after you for the generations to come, to be your God and the God of your descendants after you. . . ."
>
> God also said to Abraham, "As for Sarai your wife, you are no longer to call her Sarai; her name will be Sarah. I will bless her and will surely give you a son by her. I will bless her so that she will be the mother of nations; kings of peoples will come from her."
>
> GENESIS 17:1-7, 15-16

Abram inspects his reflection in the family's bronze mirror, a bit taken aback by his beard this morning.[5] He can still remember salt-and-pepper gray creeping into the youthful obsidian black—when had it become as pure white as sheep's wool? He wonders—if he pulled back and smoothed his crow's feet and forehead wrinkles, could he catch a faded glimpse of that younger man? He smiles. Sarai swears she sees Abram's younger self all the time, especially when he lights up while telling others about the wild adventure God has had him on.

But Abram is not a young man anymore. Next year, he'll mark a century of life. His neck and back are noticeably stiffer these days. His once-taut arm muscles quiver when he carries an animal sacrifice to the temple. Abram momentarily wonders if he'll be strong enough to hold the baby, the son that God promised him. And, as he does almost every day, Abram questions when that day will arrive. He and Sarai aren't getting any younger, and it *has* been a while, he realizes, since God last showed up—nearly five years ago.

As Abram makes his way to the front of his tent, he reflects on the day God first appeared to him, almost twenty-five years ago. That day changed so much in Abram's life—his location, his destination, even the way he follows God. Sometimes, Abram has faithfully stayed the course and honored God, but other times—Abram winces at the thought—he hasn't lived so holy. Yet Adonai, constant Adonai, has been faithful and true.

Abram stands firm on that one foundation: God's promises never falter. God will do what he says he will do.

The aging man steps out of the tent—and suddenly, *he is here*. The powerful presence—the extraordinary voice—emanating from nowhere and everywhere at once . . . Abram is stunned, jolted. He immediately recognizes that strange and lovely Voice. The eternal, ageless Voice; the Voice of love, justice, righteousness, perfection, authority, beauty, and creativity. Overwhelmed by the weight of it all, Abram falls flat on his face.

And God? Well, God doesn't mess around with small talk.

"This is my covenant with you. I will make you the father of many," the Almighty declares. "I am also going to change your name. Your name will no longer be Abram because Abram is a father. My son, you are no longer just a father. From this point forward, you will be called Abraham because now you are the father of many nations. I will bless you with this rich land and many descendants."

Abram can barely breathe. The gritty soil underneath him—the soil that is now his and his children's, and his great-great grandchildren's—seems to surge, as if the ground itself is bending and bowing in worship. Abram, overcome, can do nothing more than stay still, silent, and worshipful.

"*Abraham*, hear your new name on my lips. Soak it in. Internalize it. Because with your new name, I am changing your very identity. I am going to make you extremely fruitful. Do you understand this? Generation upon generation, stars upon stars, heirs upon heirs, my very own people will come through you."

Abram—no, *Abraham*—feels like he might burst out into song. But God isn't finished speaking.

"Sarai, your wife, is very important to me as well. I am also going to change her name. She will no longer be Sarai, *princess*. From now on, she will be known to all as Sarah, noblewoman. Sarah, mother of nations. Sarah, matriarch of kings. This is her new name and her new identity."

Abraham stays low, as the significance of all that God has said—the goodness of who Elohim is—sinks in. Quickly, though, he gets flabbergasted by his emotion and unexpectedly erupts into laughter. "How will all of this be possible?" Abraham is in a mix of absolute delight and total disbelief. "I am almost one hundred years old! Sarah is ninety! There is no possible way!"

But God has spoken. It will be as God has said. God's promises, God's blessings, and God's new names for Abraham and Sarah? Those remain.

Because when God renames, God transforms identities and purposes—permanently.

Hosea and Gomer's Children

> Yet the time will come when Israel's people will be like
> the sands of the seashore—too many to count! Then, at
> the place where they were told, "You are not my people,"
> it will be said, "You are children of the living God." Then
> the people of Judah and Israel will unite together. They
> will choose one leader for themselves, and they will return
> from exile together. What a day that will be—the day
> of Jezreel—when God will again plant his people in his
> land.
>
> In that day you will call your brothers Ammi—"My
> people." And you will call your sisters Ruhamah—"The
> ones I love."
>
> HOSEA 1:10–2:1, NLT

The prophet Hosea has a hauntingly hard call on his life. The very first time they spoke, God commanded Hosea to choose, pursue, marry, and continually love an unfaithful woman, a prostitute by trade. God, it seems, has big plans for Hosea's marriage—it is meant to be an image, an icon, a living illustration of God's love for his own unfaithful people.

So the prophet obeyed without question and married Gomer, a woman who continually returns to her trade, bringing Hosea social shame and personal heartache.

Hosea knows that his own life has been a breeze compared to his wife's. He shudders to think about the fact that she was likely sold into the sex trade as a young girl, spending her days as a sexual and economic commodity—trafficked, subjugated, and dehumanized. Gomer, a young woman in a deeply patriarchal world; well, there aren't adequate words for the unspeakable evil she has seen and known. So Hosea keeps reaching out, keeps loving her, keeps paying the debts she owes her lovers, and keeps bringing her home, even as her body keeps wandering outside of it.

Eventually, the couple have three children. And if you're wondering, yes, questions about their paternity have crossed the prophet's mind. But he has decided they are his. Period. He loves them and cares for them—out of obedience to God and out of pure, fatherly affection. Still, as each child is born, the prophet names the children from Jehovah's own heartbreak and anger, as he is instructed to do; they are named to represent Northern Israel's unfaithfulness.

- Hosea and Gomer's first son is named Jezreel, after the site of that terrible massacre, when God broke Israel's military power and independence, removing (unplanting) them from the land.

- Their second child, a bright and delightful daughter, is called Lo-Ruhamah, meaning "Not Loved" or "No Mercy."

- Their third child, another strapping baby boy, is named Lo-Ammi, meaning "Not My People."

Hosea is able to go through with it all—loving his wounded wife, naming his children in this intolerable way—because he knows, he trusts, he has faith that God has a greater plan, a long-term purpose. Hosea believes that all this agony will not be the end of his story, Gomer's story, his family's story, or even his people's story.

And God proves himself faithful.

God calls the Israelites to repent and return, declaring his unrestrained love for them. Then God does a miraculously kind thing. He gives Jezreel, Lo-Ammi, and Lo-Ruhamah brand-new names.

- Jezreel is renamed as *Planted by God in the Land.*

- Lo-Ruhamah, "Not Loved," or No Mercy: Her name is changed to *The One I Love* (Hosea 2:22-23).

- Lo-Ammi, "Not My People," is renamed as *You Are Children of the Living God.*

In declaring these new names over Hosea and Gomer's children, God simultaneously displays a new, defining reality: God is always writing a larger redemption story over his people. Amid their unfaithfulness to him, God's love and God's restoration knows no bounds. God's love is a fresh start. His love is a fragrant forest. His love is deep soil. His love is a fruitful, evergreen tree. His love is protective shade (Hosea 14:4-7).

What Hosea *doesn't* know is just how famous his children's renaming story will become—influencing the next generation, and the next, and the next. Many years later, long after Hosea and Gomer have come and gone, a faithful follower named Peter (a man also renamed by God; see John 1:35-44), will use the names of Hosea and Gomer's children to describe other future God followers: "Once you were not a people, but now you are the people of God; once you had not received mercy, but now you have received mercy" (1 Peter 2:10).

But what Hosea *does* know is that God never intends his children to carry false or undignified names forever.

Because when God renames, God redeems and writes a new story—profoundly.

Jacob

Jacob was left alone, and a man wrestled with him
till daybreak. When the man saw that he could not
overpower him, he touched the socket of Jacob's hip so
that his hip was wrenched as he wrestled with the man.
Then the man said, "Let me go, for it is daybreak."

But Jacob replied, "I will not let you go unless you
bless me."

The man asked him, "What is your name?"

"Jacob," he answered.

Then the man said, "Your name will no longer be
Jacob, but Israel, because you have struggled with God
and with humans and have overcome."

Jacob said, "Please tell me your name."

But he replied, "Why do you ask my name?" Then he
blessed him there.

So Jacob called the place Peniel, saying, "It is
because I saw God face to face, and yet my life was
spared."

GENESIS 32:24-30

Jacob, the deceiver, is terrified. He hasn't seen his brother Esau
since betraying him all those years ago. And now, on the night
before their reunion, Jacob has just received word that Esau is
coming to meet him . . . with a full-blown army.

Jacob has been hoping for reconciliation but is not so arrogant
or foolish to think it will come without a fight. Still, Jacob pauses
to beg God—the God of his father Isaac and the God of his grandfather Abraham—to keep him and his family safe.

In a show of good faith, Jacob sends some messengers ahead of him with gifts that, with any bit of luck, will appease Esau. And just in case things go awry, Jacob leads his family to a secure spot for the night. But Jacob stays by himself, setting up camp near the Jabbok River, and tries, restlessly, to fall asleep. Then, as if this crazy night could get any more stressful, a man—a stranger—shows up out of nowhere to pick a fight.

This fighting man is so resilient and unyielding that he and Jacob wind up wrestling over the course of the entire night. And though the stranger is clearly the stronger opponent, Jacob isn't a quitter. So, at morning's light, the mysterious man injures Jacob's hip—an effortless move that reveals the seriousness of his might.

And though Jacob's pain is searing, the ache pales in comparison to the realization: He has been wrestling someone extraordinary. This is not just any man. This is the face of God, or maybe an angel, or some other godly representative. So Jacob, who once stole his father's blessing through trickery and deceit, seizes this opportunity. This time, he directly demands a blessing.

Surprisingly, the man honors Jacob's request, but not in the way you'd expect. He blesses Jacob with a new name. (Because new names, after all, are great blessings.)

"What is your name?" the god-man asks.

"Jacob."

"Not anymore. From now on, you will be called Israel, because you have fought with God and with men and have won."

With that, the stranger disappears and Jacob, *Israel*, limps on his injured hip toward the Jabbok River to splash water on his face. He cups his hands to take in a long, refreshing drink. As he does, an insight startles him.

Jabbok means "emptying." Jacob knows that any of his servants or family members would hear what Jacob heard when he said the name aloud. In the twin names of Jacob and Jabbok, the hard *c/k* sound and the *b* sound are inverted. In other words, in wrestling with this god-man that night, Jacob somehow also wrestled down a mirror-image version of himself—his false self, his sinful self, his deceiver self.

Perhaps his grandfather Abraham and his grandmother Sarah's name-change story resounds through his mind. Perhaps he wonders, *Has God, at last, emptied me of my deceiver identity?* There at Jabbok, of all the places in the world, Jacob has come to the end of himself. He has become Israel instead. God has removed his false identity and blessed him with a new one in its place. And what Israel will find out soon is that God is not only restoring him but is also about to heal his relationship with his brother.

Because when God renames, God blesses and restores, powerfully.

Your Forward Name

God is the only being whose speech cannot be separated from his acts. When God renamed Abram and Sarai, he propelled them into a vast calling. When God renamed Gomer and Hosea's children, he showed his people a vision of a better future and a certain reality. When God renamed Jacob, he stripped him of what was holding him back so he could move forward into God's purposes.

When God changes your name, he brings you into his healing power and holy plans. He changes your entire story.

In place of the damaging names you have carried, the Holy Spirit, as in the ancient days, wants to speak a new name—a forward name and a freeing name—over you. God is inviting you to shed your false names, leave them behind, and replace them with his name for you.

What would happen if you and your community began to pray about, listen for, and invite God to reveal, remove, and replace any adverse names you are living under? What would that look like? Feel like?

I don't know what false names or nicknames you've been speaking over yourself or listening to, but I can say this: You are not Mistake, Idiot, Too Much, Too Little, Piggy, Overlooked, or Unloved.

You are Beloved. You are Noble. You are Spiritual Mother, Spiritual Father to Many. You are Servant of King Jesus. You are Daughter of God, Son of God. You are Renamed.

Don't listen to any names other than the ones God calls you.

And also this: If, over time, God seems to be silent about your (re)name, don't lose heart. Move toward him anyway. God may have a very specific name to speak over you in a sacred, surprising moment. Or God may be directing a long process of calling forth a name for you. Or you may already be perfectly named. Or God may wait until you meet him face-to-face.

What I'm saying is, don't get too concerned or stuck searching for some "secret" name that God may or may not reveal to you today or tomorrow or even a decade from now. God is not playing hide-and-seek with you. Isaiah 56:5 tells us that the name God will give his children is an everlasting one, a name that will never disappear. In his perfect timing, in his perfect way, he names his children.

I recently caught up with the woman we prayed for that powerful day. She told me that she hosted a birthday party for herself. Guess what name was on her cake?

My Beautiful One, written in frosting, covered in sprinkles, and decorated with delight.

Being named only matters because of the one who has named us. His name covers us; his name defines us. His name remakes us. The true and final name, the *decisive* name that God will bless you with, is one that can never be changed or taken away—because you are his.

PART II

WHOSE YOU ARE

When someone duly appreciates his or
her own existence as created in God's
image, the groundwork is in place for
that person to learn to view and treat
everyone as created in God's image.

JOHN F. KILNER

OUR NAMES CARRY WITHIN THEM a divine capacity: the knowledge that we belong somewhere and, more importantly, to Someone. You belong—heart, soul, mind, and strength—to the God who created you and gave his life to save you and call you by his name.

God has named us, uniquely and creatively—but none of our names matter apart from him, apart from how he has made us in his image and called us his children. The transformative power in our names come from him. Understanding and internalizing the dignity and destiny we have as God's image and likeness-bearing children transforms our entire sense of meaning and purpose.

Who we are matters deeply to God.

But *Whose* we are is everything.

7

GOD'S CHILD

Recognizing God's Voice

If anyone takes a human life, that person's life will also be taken by human hands. For God made human beings in his own image.

GENESIS 9:6, NLT

We have to name things rightly in order to heal from them.
We have to name things for what they are and what they do
and what they cause, in order to find freedom from them.
Jesus calls us children of God. In difficult situations . . . , we
have to make a choice. Are we going to live into and from
that name?

"IS THIS HOW GOD SPEAKS TO HIS CHILDREN?"

I am hanging out in a small meeting room on a college campus after speaking to a room full of scholars and students this morning. In this room are the actual people who helped translate and compile certain versions of THE BIBLE. That's worth mentioning because although I'm a graduate student and a lover of learning, I stayed up way too late last night binge-watching old episodes of Carpool Karaoke on YouTube and listening to some songs from, shall we say, not the most highbrow of musicians. As a result, a teensy part of me wonders if I actually belong here among BIBLE SCHOLARS. But I remind myself that they hired me, and thankfully, the talk was well received. I'm grateful.

I stand behind a generic-looking plastic table, selling books and chatting with attendees. It's exciting to interact with these thought leaders, academics whose books I've read and learned from, people who've shaped me as a preacher, pastor, and practitioner.

The line progresses until the last person—a bearded and bespectacled professor, perhaps in his early sixties—stands before me. Dew drops of sweat drizzle across his forehead because, apparently, he's "raced across campus." He tells me this bit of information and also informs me that he heard me speak this morning but was just now sitting in his office debating if he should stop by the book signing. He wasn't planning to attend, initially, but felt drawn—no, "urged"—by God to race across campus to be here now. "God told me that I couldn't let you get on a plane tonight without giving you a gift."

With that, he plops a thick and heavy-looking book down in front of me. The flimsy table visibly shakes at its heft. "Wow!" I exclaim, responding to the enormous thud. "Thank you! How thoughtful."

I glance down at the hardcover book and notice immediately that it's not just any book; it's a book with his name on it. *Well, this is odd*, I think. But okay, maybe he wants to exchange his book for mine—a swapping of *our* literary work. Then I notice what his book is about: common mistakes that public speakers and Bible teachers make. Ouch.

Surely this sixty-year-old man, a professional in his field, a professional in my field, hasn't sweated and slogged this book across campus just to teach me a lesson, as if I'm one of his students. He's still standing in front of me, expecting me to say more, but I'm currently suspended between mixed emotions—wanting to give this guy grace and simultaneously realizing what this book is, what this incident is. Not actually a gift, as he described it, but an insult masked as one.

"Well, thank you again, sir," I finally respond demurely, my southern upbringing coming in handy. "I certainly hope this isn't a hint for me. Ha . . . ha . . . ha."

He starts to speak again. Then stops himself, picks up my book off the table, and flips it over to peruse the back cover, as if he's considering buying it. But he sets it down and suddenly looks resolved. It's as if, if he doesn't say this one thing, he might never speak again. He opens his mouth, and I brace myself.

"You don't use the Bible well. You speak with slogans. You could learn a thing or two from my book. You should read it before you agree to do something like this again." Double ouch.

In the study of linguistics there is something known as speech-act theory, where it's generally agreed that words not only say things; they do things. A classic example of speech-act theory is a bride and groom saying the words "I do." They've exchanged vows and changed their lives.

Most speech acts can be broken down into at least three layers of communication: (1) locution—what is said; (2) illocution—what is meant by what is said; (3) perlocution—what the speaker's words do to the hearer. Allow me to break down the speech act that is happening in front of me at this very moment.

- *Locution* (what is said): "God told me to tell you that you don't use the Bible well. You speak with slogans, etc."
- *Illocution* (what is meant): "You shouldn't be here."
- *Perlocution* (what his words do): I am the beads of sweat on his forehead, small and annoying, something to be wiped away.

Just like that, I'm shrinking. His words have accomplished exactly what he intended them to. And the worst part, perhaps even worse than his arrogance, is that I'm allowing it to happen.

Tough skin. Tender heart. Tough skin. Tender heart. Tough skin. Tender heart. My mantra. As a woman in public speaking, a woman in the preaching world, a woman in leadership, I've had to develop resiliency. There are a lot of opinions about how I should be doing my job—and even more opinions about whether I should be doing my job at all. I once had a stranger on Facebook send me messages upon messages of Pauline verses informing me that I am the reason the church is falling apart. (I was tempted to send him every verse in Deuteronomy about crushed testicles. Instead, I chose my motto: Tough skin; tender heart.) I ignored and blocked him.

I feel it's important to be clear for myself as much as for you, reader, that the hurt I feel from this interaction isn't about a theological position. Though I stand firmly rooted in a local church and Christian community that allows women to exercise all of their spiritual gifts in every church office, I have dearly loved friends, family members, and partners in ministry on different spots along that particular theological spectrum.

So this is not that. Or at least not only that.

This man has managed to go right through my tough skin into my deep tissue. He's touched the nervous system, inflamed it. My brain is wildly sending signals, bright, hot flashes of pain, to my inner little girl. She's already convinced she doesn't measure up. She came here today completely nervous about being out of her element. But now? It's official. Declared. Named. An urgent message from a biblical scholar, no less.

Here's the thing. On one hand, I know I don't have to listen to or internalize his opinion. But on the other hand, what if he's right? What if I am a fraud? What if I do handle the Bible incorrectly? What if I do use slogans? What if I shouldn't have come here? What if this was a word from God, a warning from God to stop speaking, stop doing this thing I feel like God has called and designed me to do?

This scholar is still standing at my book table awkwardly, waiting for a reply. But what can I actually, seriously say in this moment without giving my vulnerability away to him? Without giving him too much power? What can I say that will make this whole interaction just disappear?

I'm starting to rage, I realize, beginning to Hulk out on the inside, but I'm desperate to remain Scarlett O'Hara on the outside. Stay polite and charming before I start smashing desks and chalkboards and/or break into hysterical sobs. So I checklist through the next few moments just to get away as fast as possible.

- Say pleasantries. ✓
- Check time on phone. ✓
- Excuse self to catch flight. ✓
- Stuff his book in my bag. ✓
- Walk across room and thank host for a lovely weekend. ✓
- Escape building. ✓
- Run to rental car. ✓
- Proceed with meltdown. ✓✓✓✓✓✓✓

I sit in my car, warming the engine, fighting back tears. I told you earlier that Aubrey means "ruler with wisdom," and sometimes, by the grace of God and the Spirit's power in my life, I live up to that namesake. But other times, I cry in rental cars. *Try to let this go*, I tell myself. *Tough skin; tender heart.*

Once, my son asked me if God is bigger than a house. "Yes," I replied, "In a way."

"Bigger than a statue?"

"Definitely."

"But can he also become teeny-tiny, small enough to fit inside of a mouse's mouth?"

"I hope so," I replied.

God, if you are able, please crawl inside this mouse's-mouth moment with me right now. I need you here in this small space.

Dust Brothers and Sisters

Genesis tells us that if anyone takes a human life, that person's life will also be taken by human hands. "For God made human beings." We are also told that humans are made from the dirt. In fact, the name *human* or "man" is actually connected to the terms "red stuff," "of the ground."[1]

This brings to mind a moment in the life of Jesus when a bloodthirsty crowd, intent on humiliating if not murdering an adulterous woman, wanted to trap Jesus into saying something unlawful. "Teacher," they cried, "this woman was caught in the act of adultery. The law of Moses says to stone her. What do you say?" (John 8:4-5, NLT).

This story gives us a grave picture of the perverting nature of sin, as God's own image bearers are hell-bent on destroying the image of God in each other—and in God himself.

While the crowd waited impatiently for his answer, Jesus slowed the moment down. He stooped to the ground and spent a few moments scrawling in the dust with his finger. This act is such a physical and spiritual act at once—the Son of God squatting, writing in the dust. Can you imagine what the crowd must have been thinking? I have so many questions.

Was Jesus praying? Was he listening to the Spirit for direction?

Was he considering his options? I'm even curious if Jesus was trying to make a connection for the crowd—to their shared humanity. *We all come from dust, and to dust we shall return.*

Perhaps he wanted the hyped-up mob to realize that they and this woman were not so different. All of them were born from the same dirt, saints and sinners alike. Was Jesus heartbroken as he caressed the dirt his Father created? The same dirt used to create these humans who were now treating one of their own like dirt?

Swiss theologian Karl Barth wrote, "We have to think of *every human being*, even the oddest, most villainous or miserable, as one to whom Jesus Christ is Brother and God is Father."[2] Was this Jesus' point? This woman is your dust sister, MY dust sister, and yet you're treating her like a villain, like your enemy.

At last, Jesus stood up and addressed the crowd. "Okay," he said, "You want to murder this woman? Fine. If any of you are sinless, go ahead. Start throwing stones."

The irony, of course? Jesus alone was sinless; Jesus alone had the right to judge.

Another irony? The people, this riled-up crowd, truly thought they were right. They believed they were condemning her with God's approval, with God's voice. But then came Jesus, who *actually* spoke to her with God's voice. He showed her exactly how God speaks to his children.

And perhaps the deepest irony was that later—for this woman, for this angry mob, for you and for me—Jesus would bear the judgment, "the stones," of the Cross.

All this woman knew that day was this: The redemption of God shared space with her name. Moments before, her name was condemned. But Jesus renamed her Not Condemned (John 8:11).

When God renames his children throughout Scripture, we discover that he is also changing their identities and purposes. God is so powerful that his speech is tantamount to his act. There is no separating the two; God's speech *is* God's act. And so, through this divine speech act over the condemned woman, Jesus did two things simultaneously: He named her Free, and he *set* her free.

Children of God

Though the professor at my book table didn't come close to throwing stones, he has hurt me, and the following week I still haven't let it go. I'm officially that obsessive person who has imaginary conversations in the shower, the car, and the bathroom.

I've replayed that moment with him probably eight thousand times, like a needle stuck in a record groove. Each time it circles around, I grow wittier, more inspired, and, frankly, incredible at wrecking him—blatantly ignoring Jesus' warnings about speaking contemptuously about others. *Lord, Jesus Christ, have mercy on me, a sinner.*

Because I can't seem to move on, I am currently sitting cross-legged on the floor of a friend's office, going over the event, asking what part of the professor's advice I should hear.

What should I take in? What should I ignore? Should I read his book? I'm still carrying it around in my bag. I should probably take it out and open it but haven't been able to bring myself to do so. I've just been lugging it around with me—and every time I lift my purse, I'm reminded of the weight this whole situation has over me, pulling on my neck, pinching my nerves.

My friend waits patiently as I vomit my mixed feelings before her. I tell her all about my imaginary conversations and the witty comebacks. But then I finally feel brave enough to ask the question that's really underlying it all.

"What if he's right? What if this is a message from God?"

"Aubrey, can I ask you something?" she replies, gently.

"Sure."

"Are you a child of God?" She's asking kindly, not condescendingly. She's reminding me who I am. Reminding me of what I know, my true name.

"Yes," I whisper.

"Is this how God speaks to his children?"

Of course not, I think.

"How does God speak to his children?"

"With dignity," I reply. "With compassion. With love."

"Exactly," she says. "If God wants you to hear something, God's going to say it in a way that you would actually hear—in his voice—with grace, in a way that doesn't condemn or shame you."

What I realize right then and there on her office floor is that there is a difference between going under the knife of a surgeon you trust and being stabbed in the alley by a stranger. "It sounds like you were stabbed in the alley," she adds as I say this thought aloud, "and now you're asking what you did to deserve it."

We can wreck each other with our speech acts, or we can be this for each other—the actual body of Christ, reaching into the fragile places with healing.

We take some time to be quiet and pray together. I close my eyes, and God brings to mind an image. I am standing on the front steps of the college where I spoke. I have glass shards stuck all over my body—my arms, my legs, my head. God gently removes each one. Then he offers me a robe—a graduation robe, but it's warm and comforting, more like a bathrobe. *This is what I designed you to wear*, I sense God saying. *Not those shards of shame but the clothing I have for you.*

On my drive home from my friend's office, I think of the prophet Ezekiel. He had a message from God—a painful one—but he spent over a year lying on his side, on the dirt, in front of his people (Ezekiel 3:26; 4:4-6); he humbled himself, he suffered in front of the Israelites—earning his right to be their prophet. Perhaps most noteworthy: Ezekiel did this *before* he ever opened his mouth to correct them.

I consider Ezekiel and realize that I would have loved to learn from this professor had he earned the right to be a prophetic voice in my life. But he didn't. He didn't have the relational credit. I can forgive him for what happened, and I will; still, he doesn't have power or authority over me. I also realize something more. For perhaps the first time in this entire event, I realize that I am angry. Just not at myself.

I am angry that the system in which I have lived and served for decades still finds it acceptable for a male colleague to tear a female colleague down, and I'm furious that I have been socialized to blame myself for it. I am angry that in that one conversation this man got to be a whole person, taking up as much space as he wanted, while I was left to retreat, to shrink into oblivion. And I'm even more angry because this moment was a microcosm of every moment when someone has been unable to manage their own ego but blamed another person for it—while simultaneously masking *that* as spirituality. I'm sure I'm guilty of it as well, but I would still venture to say that God is angry about that too.

We have to name things rightly in order to heal from them. We have to name things for what they are and what they do and what they cause, in order to find freedom from them. Jesus calls us children of God (Luke 20:36). In difficult situations like these, we have to make a choice. Are we going to live into and from that name?

As for me, I will respond to this situation by holding onto my name as God's Child. I will choose Jesus' victory, not shame's defeat.

So when I arrive home, I finally take the book out of my purse. I'd be lying if I said I wasn't curious about its content, but that curiosity is overruled by a new conviction. There is absolutely nothing in this for me.

I walk to the garage and open the lid to our blue recycling bin; it's overflowing with Amazon and Target boxes, so I lean over it and press all of my weight, all of my anger, onto the book, compacting it down as far as it will possibly go, releasing my anger and shame into God's care.

———•———

In another interaction between Jesus and a woman, he appears to Mary Magdalene after his resurrection (John 20:11-18). He was like her in body but also so transformed that she didn't recognize her own Lord, her own friend, her own Savior.

But then.

He spoke her name.

And it did something.

Mary woke up, finally realizing that her brilliant, resurrected, victorious-over-the-grave King was the same man in front of her, calling her name.

This is what I know: When our enemy tries to defeat us, beat us, defame us, or shrink us, we fight our battles from resurrection not destruction. We fight our false names in the name above all other names. There is no greater weapon, no greater power.

May you hear Jesus whisper, "Neither do I condemn you. Go and live a life of righteousness." And may you listen for the true names he speaks over you.

This is how God speaks to his children.

8

GOD'S LIVING STATUES

Our Iconoclast God

Then God said, "Let us make human beings in our image, to be like us. They will reign over the fish in the sea, the birds in the sky, the livestock, all the wild animals on the earth, and the small animals that scurry along the ground."

GENESIS 1:26, NLT

God, who stands wholly opposed to any graven images or false idols—God, who for all intents and purposes is an iconoclast—allows himself to be represented by living, breathing images: you and me. The infinite God chose to make for himself embodied agents in finite, physical, and imperfect human beings. In other words, *you are God's living statue*.

MY PARENTS SENT ME to a private high school where the boys wore pleated khaki pants; leather, braided belts; and tucked-in golf shirts. Basically, the boys at my school generally dressed and acted like my dad.

So when I met a group of skater boys from the local public school, I was instantly starry-eyed. With their green mohawks and their tattoos and their punk-rock-band T-shirts—well, they were basically a poor man's (a sheltered sixteen-year-old's) demigod. Hercules and Achilles come to life wearing chain wallets and Vans shoes.

I desperately wanted these guys to think I was cool.

Whenever I think back on this time in my life, I am reminded of a quote from the famous Rabbi Zusya: "In the coming world, they will not ask me: 'Why were you not Moses?' They will ask me: 'Why were you not Zusya?'"[1] When I contextualize Rabbi Zusya's question—*Why were you not Aubrey?*—my gut answers with a wrenching memory involving that skater squad . . . and the 1990s pop-rock sensation Hootie and the Blowfish.

Let me explain.

Young Aubrey saved up some of her babysitting money to purchase the latest Hootie and the Blowfish album, which included her favorite song at the time, a wildly popular tune, "Hold My Hand." She raced over to the skater squad's hangout spot to play them her new favorite song. (This was the 1990s, and also the suburbs, so the hangout spot was most definitely a coffee shop near a skate park.)

Seems innocent enough, right?

Even now as I'm typing this, adult Aubrey is cringing, wanting to bend space and time to stop her younger self. I want to blockade that coffee-shop door with yellow caution tape, padlocks, and dead bolts. I want to yell, "Run away, youngblood!"

Nonetheless, teen Aubrey strutted confidently inside the coffee shop with her brand-new Hootie CD and her portable CD player. She plopped down on a leather couch next to her friends—who were, by the way, smoking cigarettes and drinking coffee (at age sixteen! Where were the parents in the 1990s?)—and started playing them her new favorite song.

Just as Hootie arrived at his most passionate refrain—"I wanna run with you / won't you let me run with you? Yeah."—

—they started laughing.

And they kept laughing.

And then they began ripping young Aubrey to shreds. "Ohhhh, you like Hootie and the Blowfish. Do you like other Top 40 songs too?"

Top 40, padawan Aubrey learned that fateful day, was a big no-no among angsty, punk-rock 1990s teenagers.

Though she wanted to ignore them and defiantly turn the music up even louder, the stakes were too high. Their opinion mattered way too much, and this incident wouldn't be the last of the embarrassment she would feel around them. Frankly, she didn't have the kind of nerve it takes to fight back yet. That ire will come as she gets older (and develops a broader taste in music), but not yet, not on this tender today.

Instead, young Aubrey excused herself to the bathroom, snuck out the coffee shop's back door, and drove home, her head bowed low by humiliation.

———

I have a colleague and friend, the leader of an award-winning global enterprise, no less, someone you'd never expect to wrestle with her *identity*, who says she's always just one thought away from shame. She has to constantly fill herself up with God's names for her—Loved, Accepted, Worthy, Leader.

My husband, a senior pastor and church planter, says something similar; the gap for him lies between the confident apostle that he is and the grown man with self-doubt he also is. He's continually reminding himself of his true names—Brother of Christ, Approved Of.

And me, now a full-fledged grown-up—on most days, I walk with my head held high. But in my more vulnerable moments, it's exasperating how quickly I can revert to that teenage version of myself in the coffee shop, so exposed, so rejected. Like a kid in an oversized trench coat and deerstalker hat, I sometimes feel like an imposter, just pretending to be a confident adult.

I forget who I belong to. I forget that I bear the image of God in my very bones, and breath, and being.

The secret, I think, is that most of us feel that way now and then.

The Image of God

The phrase *image of God*, often referred to as *imago Dei*, comes out of the very first book of the Bible. In Genesis 1:26, after creating the whole world from nothing, God turns his attention to something extraordinary: "Let us make human beings in our image, to be like us," God declares. "They will reign over the fish in the sea, the birds in the sky, the livestock, all the wild animals on the earth, and the small animals that scurry along the ground" (NLT).

In the ancient Near East, where the literature and stories of Genesis were born, a lot of folks believed that images contained the substance of whatever they represented. So basically, a whole bunch of kings and rulers stationed statues or icons of themselves in certain places or territories, as a way of declaring their presence (their control and rule) there.

But it wasn't so much the physical likeness of the image that mattered, though that was certainly part of its value. The image's *essence* was key. These statues or icons were thought to contain the very soul and authority of whoever they represented.[2] In other words, statues and icons served not just as placeholders but as actual, embodied delegates.

So when we come across the word *image* in Genesis 1:26 ("Let us make human beings in our image, to be like us" [NLT]), translated from the Hebrew word *ṣelem* or *tselem*, meaning idol or statue, we get a glimpse of what God is up to.

What we discover is this astounding piece of information: God, who stands wholly opposed to any graven images or false idols (Exodus 20:4-6)—God, who for all intents and purposes is an iconoclast—allows himself to be represented by living, breathing images: you and me. The infinite God chose to make for himself embodied agents in finite, physical, and imperfect human beings. In other words, *you are God's living statue.*

You are here to represent and reflect God's *essence*—his presence, power, and compassion, on this earth. As Peter says, "You are living stones that God is building into his spiritual temple" (1 Peter 2:5, NLT).

You are a living, breathing delegate of the Kingdom of God.

Of course, the reality is, we are all a bit broken, a little bit insecure teenager, in the way we name ourselves and the way we display God's image. But that changes nothing about who we are. We are God's handmade *tselem*, his iconic *imago*.

In fact, if we look a bit earlier in Genesis chapter 1, we read a songlike description of God creating the world, and we hear this repeated refrain: *Let there be. Let there be. Let there be.*

- Let there be light.
- Let there be a vast sky.
- Let there be wild, exquisite oceans.
- Let there be kale, strawberries, green beans, and sweet peaches.
- Let there be stars for romance and guidance.
- Let there be sun and moons and massive, mysterious planets.
- Let there be salmon and narwhals.

- Let there be tiny hummingbirds and cherry-red cardinals, and, of course, fireflies and butterflies.

Let there be were the whispered words of wisdom from God's song of creation.

But then, God startles us. God interrupts his own song and his own creative process to do and say a new thing: *Let us make.*[3]

Humanity, distinct from the rest of creation, is not a spoken word poem. We are something else entirely, a new kind of God art, not called forth into existence but made. Humans were designed and sculpted as God's *tselem*, his living statues, with divine definition and holy precedence.

Unique from everything else that exists, we reflect God to the world around us—again, not as a symbol but as an actual, personified agent of God's Kingdom.

This is your birthright dignity and destiny, bestowed upon you by God himself: You have within your ancient bloodlines, your ancestral bones, your creation skin, and your exquisite God-made-ness an explosive amount of image-bearing potential and possibility.

So, on the days you find yourself reverting to your inner teenager—and those days will come—never grow weary in claiming your God-givenness. Never grow passive about smashing up the false images and false names inside of you.

Even if you aren't perfect (you aren't), even if you are *not* beyond criticism (which is an impossible goal to meet, by the way), even if you're not like that other person (you aren't supposed to be), even if you have a whole list of reasons for putting on that trench coat and disqualifying yourself (I hope you don't, but these heads and hearts of ours get noisy), even if you've been passed up or overlooked (I know, it hurts)—even in all the endless "even ifs"—God has ground for you to take and chains for you to break as his living statue, for his name, his glory, and his Kingdom.

So, turn your music up a little louder and shine your light with determination and delight. The world needs to see God's image in you—because the world needs to see God.

———✦———

Years ago, one of the skater boys called me up on the phone. He had been through a major life crisis and was doing some self-reflection. "I'm sorry for how I treated you then," he said. "I was a stupid teenager and didn't know any better. But it wasn't cool, and I know it hurt. Will you forgive me?"

I realize this is sort of a cliché experience, but I also know that he was daring to express the *imago Dei* inside of himself. My adult self and my sixteen-year-old self both recognized that. So we answered his question with a resounding yes.

Sometimes, situations of embarrassment, shame, or rejection become a question: "Will you, in spite of this difficult thing that happened, continue to take up space, continue to assert yourself? Will you come back to life? Will you bring your full self to the table once more? Will you own the image of God in you, even when it's painful? Will you show up here as God's representative?"

I hope you say yes—an audacious, auspicious, unapologetic yes—every single time.

9

GOD'S LIKENESS
The Spitting Image

This is the written account of Adam's family line.
When God created [humankind], he made them in the
likeness of God. . . .
When Adam had lived 130 years, he had a son in his own
likeness, in his own image; and he named him Seth.

GENESIS 5:1, 3

**You are the spitting image of God, breathed to life from
God's own breath, born from the DNA of his superb
creativity, crafted from his hands, cradled in his heart,
and brought to life on earth in order to reflect his image
wherever you go.**

"OH MY GOODNESS! Aren't you just the spitting image of your mom?"

My fourteen-year-old son hears this all the time. He handles it graciously, but can you imagine being a teenage boy, burgeoning into a man, constantly being told you look exactly like your forty-year-old mother? I mean, *I* know he's lucky to get my good looks, but I'm not totally sure he agrees.

The phrase *spitting image* alludes to someone who looks so much like another person, it's as if they were expectorated into existence straight from their look-alike's saliva. The term allegedly came into circulation around 1689 when playwright George

Farquhar used it in his play *Love and a Bottle*. "Poor child!" the line goes. "He's as like his own dada as if he were spit out of his mouth."[1]

A more posh way to put this is the word *likeness*—the idea that someone so strongly resembles someone else, it's like looking at a picture.

And that, Genesis tells us, is what we are: "When God created [humankind], he made them in the likeness of God" (Genesis 5:1).

We are the spitting image of God.

Typically, whenever we talk about, debate, or consider what it means that humans are made in the image and likeness of God, we look at characteristics or attributes. Now of course, some of God's characteristics are simply and wholly his—his omniscience, omnipresence, self-existence, eternality. But many of God's other characteristics are already true and become increasingly true about us, as we are made more like Christ through the power of the Holy Spirit.

We are like God in that we rule creation.

We are like God in our creativity.

We are like God in our relationships.

We are like God in that we are unlike animals.

We become like God in our mercy.

We become like God in our love.

We become like God in our holiness.

We become like God in our justice.

But Genesis 5:3 offers us a clue to help us better answer this question—*What does it mean that humans have been made in the image and likeness of God?* "When Adam had lived 130 years, he had a son in his own likeness, in his own image; and he named him Seth" (Genesis 5:3).

Seth was made in the image and likeness of his dad, Adam. So naturally, we assume that Seth probably *looked* like Adam, and in other ways favored Adam and acted like Adam. They probably spoke in the same dialect and scratched their beards in a similar fashion. In another life, they might have had the same taste in hip-hop music or the same affinity for piña coladas and walks in the rain.

Still, the concept of Seth's "image and likeness" is much deeper than the ways he looked and acted like Adam. The point of Seth being made in his dad's image and likeness is that Seth had a blood relationship, a familial bond, an incomparable connection with his dad.

The *image* and *likeness* of Adam that resided inside of Seth wasn't strictly a series of attributes or similarities. It was an indication of his unique and special intimacy with his father.

Seth was part of his father's family, his father's community, and his father's purposes on this planet, just as you and I, in Christ, are part of our Father's family, community, and purposes for this world.

Listen, friend: I know you've lost some battles. I know you're weary. I know you're lonely. I know your heart is prone to wander. I know you're angry. I know you wonder if you ever truly hear from God. I know you've been let down. I know you've been hurt. I know you have struggled with your name and maybe even with God's name.

But what I also know is this: Through the blood of Jesus, you have been made "blood" with God's family. You are a child of God, with all the benefits and blessings that comes from being part of his incredible family. In Jesus, you are bound with God, as God is bound, ever faithful and true, to you.

So let's explore the implications of this "spitting image" connection. We're going to go on three walks to discover how this unbreakable family bond affects how we move through the world.

Walk One: The Classical Image (Monkey Island, Oklahoma)

I am out for a walk in a rural lakeside town called Monkey Island, Oklahoma. A new golf-cart path, which leads from one side of the small island to the other, just opened up, and I'm excited to explore it.

About two miles into my walk, I notice that a small section of the newly paved sidewalk contains a series of embedded bricks, several of them engraved with inspirational quotes. The first engraving says BE BOLD in all caps. A few steps later, the next brick declares BE BRAVE. I expect the third one, in keeping with the theme, to say BE BEAUTIFUL. Instead, my foot lands on DON'T BE A WIMP. I burst out laughing.

———◆———

What bricks do we see along the theological path as we wrestle with how we carry God's image and likeness? Church history provides a few foundational—or classical—views that can be helpful as we seek to understand a fuller picture of the image of God.

- **Brick 1.** We have been created in God's image *substantively*. Old-school theologians (think fun names, like Irenaeus and Aquinas) have long believed that something about our substance or structure is like God's substance or structure. In other words, we have some capacity that makes us image bearers of God. The unfortunate downside of the substance view is, of course, that if someone is differently abled or not rational, they have been wrongly seen as less of a human being. But because we are many parts of one body (Romans 12:5), we all belong to each other and we all bring something to the *imago* table. So when understood rightly, it's actually a remarkable thing—something about our substance resembles God. If you ever doubt your value, ask the Spirit to help you internalize this—something about you beautifully resembles something beautiful about God.

- **Brick 2.** We have been created in God's image *functionally*. The image of God is something we do, as a function, as we rule over created order. We are little viceroys, little kings and queens, and *the way* we govern creation is a way we image God. The downside of the functional view is that in our sin, we've twisted "dominion" to mean doing whatever we want to whoever we want, taking advantage of positions of power, and destroying the earth. But the redemptive side of the functional view is that it highlights that we all have a purpose in God's Kingdom. Whenever you feel lost, confused, or even frustrated about your calling or purpose, consider this: You are here to cultivate your community, your family, your home, your place of work, et cetera in a way that brings order to chaos and turns your "places" into garden-like spaces where others can flourish.[2]

- **Brick 3.** We have been created in God's image *relationally*.[3] Because God's nature is a relationship (Father, Son, Spirit), we are meant to image God as we relate with others and also with God. Our relationships should reflect God's love. The downside of the relational view is that the church has tended to reduce this to only include romantic relationships or has idolized the biological family unit, resulting in pain to people outside of these categories. But we are all the *imago* because we reflect God through all kinds of wonderful, life-giving relationships. If ever you feel lonely, remember that you are invited to image God in your relational union with the Trinity and in Christian community, so you never have to be truly alone.

Walk Two: The Collective Image of God (Botswana, Africa)

Kevin and I are living and working with his mentor in Zambia, but we've taken a weekend holiday in Botswana. We're out for a lovely evening stroll when we spot something extraordinary. About twenty feet ahead, a warthog is casually bopping down the gravel sidewalk toward us.

Kevin and I, not used to African wildlife acting so unceremoniously, start making stupid jokes *at the warthog*; we actually yell things, like "Hey Pumbaa! Where's Timon?"

Then we realize something; it's not just one warthog. It's two! Two warthogs! This feels so momentous to us, we actually start jumping up and down chanting, "There's two warthogs! Two warthogs! Two warthogs!" I'm not sure who we're even saying it to, but we want to shout about it.

The warthogs aren't impressed. In fact, they actually seem to look a little, I don't know, *threatening* might be the right word. "Does it look like they're about to charge us?" I ask Kevin, whose face reflects what I feel—panicked.

We don't really know what to do. *Is this safe? Is this normal?* We aren't sure, so we opt to race across the street to the other sidewalk to allow them their space. When in doubt, give wild animals the right of way.

Now safely on the other side of the road, from our new vantage point, we spot something else—*the why* of the warthogs' anger. We've missed the big picture. It's not one warthog. It's not even two warthogs. It's a whole family of warthogs: mama, daddy, and their four little warthog babies following behind. Pumbaa and his wife were ready to protect their babies from the ridiculous American tourists.

If you thought we were excited about two warthogs, just imagine our whole-warthog-family energy. We start dancing this time and shouting even louder, "It's a warthog family! It's a warthog family! It's a warthog family!"

They just walk on by, ignoring us, much cooler than we'll ever be.

———◆———

We have a beautiful understanding as Christians, especially Western Christians, that we as individuals have been created uniquely and lovingly in God's image. The problem is that our sin (yes, we can go to our sin problem now) has caused us to miss the whole picture.

Genesis tells us, "In the image of God he created them" (Genesis 1:27). Let me repeat that with emphasis: In the image of God, he created *them*. God himself declares unequivocally that all of humanity bears his image and likeness. Yet, in our flawed attempts to focus on how each individual is *so singularly* created as *imago*, we have harmfully exalted some images as superior to others. We've neglected all the "warthogs," the whole family of God. Historically, many white American Christians have sinfully and abusively dishonored, devalued, dehumanized, and demoralized the image of God in women, in brothers and sisters of color, and in the vulnerable. This is not the heart of God.

Fourth-century theologian Gregory of Nyssa, one of the earliest opponents of the institution of slavery, asserted that all of humanity, not "any particular man," bear the image of God. All people "are alike: they equally bear in themselves the Divine image."[4]

Author Jemar Tisby expands on this truth: "God's fingerprints rest upon every single person without restriction. . . . All people equally bear the likeness of God and thus possess incalculable and inviolable value. Human beings do not simply *have* the image of

God; we *are* the image of God."[5] This means that there is no room in God's Kingdom for racial supremacy, sexism, or the marginalization of people groups.

Friend, you may have felt belittled. You may have been actively harmed because of your race, gender, or sexuality. You may also have participated, even unknowingly, in making someone else feel diminished or "less than." We have been hurt, and we hurt others, because we struggle to see the whole *imago*. But we are called and empowered by the work of the Holy Spirit to honor and affirm the image of God in all people. This requires intentionality, humility, awareness, repentance (in many cases), lament, and sacrificial love.

In his book *Fearfully and Wonderfully Made*, leprosy surgeon Dr. Paul Brand writes, "If each of us can learn to glory in the fact that we matter little except in relation to the whole, and if each will acknowledge the worth in every other member, then perhaps the cells of Christ's body will begin acting as Christ intended."[6]

The point is, though individuals are indeed image bearers, the full image of God cannot be fully revealed through one person. God has designed all of humanity *together* to reveal more of his incredible image and likeness. With all her exquisite diversity, humanity *as a whole*, *as a collective*, displays God's image. Together, in our diverse unity, we more accurately reflect God's multifaceted magnificence.

Walk Three: The Uncontaminated Image of God (Edinburgh, Scotland)

It's the summer before my senior year of college. I am out for a walk in Edinburgh, Scotland, thinking about how lucky I am to be alive right now[7] in the land of MacBeth and Nessie, kilts, and castles, when my serene stroll is momentarily disrupted by a friendly little schnauzer.

The curious puppy sniffs around my feet, then looks up at me with his puppy-schuppy-cutesy eyes, basically begging me to pet him. "I had schnauzers growing up," I say to his owner, kneeling to nuzzle the dog's furry ears. "What's his name?"

Just as I start tickling the dog's neck, his owner responds flatly, "His name's Alistair, ken? But dinnae pet him. He's got shite all over his wee face."

"Oh . . . ummm . . . eww. Thank you?"

To this day, I'm still not sure why she didn't say anything *before* I started petting little Alistair, but I yank my hand back quickly and run to the nearest public loo to wash up.

———————•

For Christians, "God created human beings in his image and likeness" is a foundational claim of our faith. And yet, I don't know how many sermons I have sat through where the pastor reminds me that the image of God in me is *so* broken and *so* wretched and *so* ruined, *so* eroded, *so* warped, *so* demolished, *so* covered in *you know what*.[8] I want to stand up and yell, "Okay! I get it. Of sinners, I am the worst. But I'm in Christ now. Can I at least start living like I am redeemed and being made new?"

Can we be clear about something concerning the image of God? Yes, sin has destroyed the way *we* bear God's image and likeness. But the first and final *imago Dei* is not a what, but a *who*—Jesus. The image of God is unbroken, unmarred, and uncontaminated.

I certainly understand what these well-meaning pastors are trying to do—remind me of my sinful nature, my depravity, so that I can comprehend what great a salvation I have in Jesus. And I never want to grow numb to his saving work over sin. I never want to grow arrogant. But I wonder and worry, frankly, about the long-term, damaging effects on Christians of being told how awful and unworthy we are all the time.

There are generations of beloved children of God—forgiven, renewed, reborn, filled with the Holy Spirit, united with Christ, more than conquerors (Romans 8:37)—who see themselves as incompetent, dirty, and unable to experience victory. Maybe you've felt this way.

Too often, we live as if we have no strength, no freedom, no power. Human beings bought with the blood of Jesus—sons and daughters who are the very image of God themselves—somehow live with a subconscious spiritual belief that we are damaged goods.

If that's you, can I remind you about one of your true names again?

You are the image and likeness of God.

The Lord has spoken dignity, delight, and destiny over you.

Apart from Jesus Christ, yes, you are a sinner, *but in Christ,* you are empowered with the resurrection power of the Holy Spirit. You are clothed in righteousness. You are declared clean. You are no longer contaminated by your former bondage to sin. As the apostle Paul reminds us, "Anyone in Christ is a new creation" (2 Corinthians 5:17, author's paraphrase).

Roughly translated?

"You know that nasty *stuff* all over your face? In Jesus—the true image of God—it's gone."

———◆———

One of the earliest female Christian writers, medieval theologian and mystic Julian of Norwich, believed that because of God's love and goodness, we are made in his likeness. In her tremendous work, *Revelations of Divine Love,* she wrote:

For [God] does not despise what he has made, nor does he disdain to serve us in the simplest task that belongs by nature to our bodies, through love of the soul which he has made in his own likeness; for as the body is clad in cloth, and the flesh in the skin, and the bones in the flesh, and the heart in the chest, so are we, soul and body, clad in the goodness of God and enclosed in it.[9]

Being made in the image and likeness of God, therefore, is *not simply* a list of divine qualities—it's a journey of discovery about the goodness of God, our Maker, who humbled himself enough to take on the very likeness he gave us so that we could become one with him. Through Jesus, you have access to relational intimacy with the God of the universe, and as his image bearer, you have value beyond compare.

You are the spitting image of God, breathed to life from God's own breath, born from the DNA of his superb creativity, crafted from his hands, cradled in his heart, and brought to life on earth in order to reflect his image wherever you go.

10

GOD'S FOUND ONE
Seen in the Wasteland

Put on your new nature, created to be like God—truly
righteous and holy.

EPHESIANS 4:24, NLT

> A "found" object . . . was once discarded but has been
> picked up, restored, and repurposed with new vision. If
> you are in a wasteland or wilderness season, God has not
> forgotten you. . . . Your name is not Lost. *You* are not lost. . . .
> You are Found, for eternal glory.

IT'S A STOVETOP-HOT SATURDAY MORNING. Despite the wretched heat
and humidity (none of which are good for my hair, my joints, my
mood, or my body odor), I'm hiking a trail at a local arboretum
to one of my favorite destinations: a quaint little cedar bench that
sits underneath a honeycomb-shaped wooden canopy.

When I was part of a theater program in undergrad, we had
this little ritual where we'd walk around the theater space and say,
This is the place where I [fill in the blank]. It was a powerful speech
act, a marking, a naming—a way to honor God through shared
memory. And this honeycomb, well, *this is the place where I sit and
connect with God.*

90

The trail to my bench is dotted with magnolia bushes and lamb's-ear plants. The forest surrounding the path is lush and mysterious, as if a unicorn might emerge from the brush at any moment. There are handmade benches here and there where a hiker can stop, rest, and breathe it all in. This wilderness enchants the soul.

After a late night's thunderstorm, however, my typically smooth and magical trail has morphed into something else—lumpy and awkward like a woodchip-mogul ski run. Fitting, because that's exactly how I feel, how the world feels, at the moment.

It is 2020. If you are reading this with any stretch of distance, emotionally or otherwise, from the events of this year, it may take you a moment to recall that with this new decade came a slew of new names: Novel Coronavirus, COVID-19, Social Distance, Shelter in Place, Asynchronous and Synchronous Learning, Zoom Fatigue, "Unprecedented."

Just a few months into the pandemic, many of us are so used to these unusual phrases; they don't even seem interesting anymore. But they are certainly life-altering, to say the least.

This year, Kevin and I lose loved ones. Our friends and neighbors lose loved ones. Strangers lose loved ones. You probably lost loved ones. And it's all devastating and bizarre.

There are other names this year, important ones: Ahmaud Arbery, George Floyd, Breonna Taylor, Jacob Blake. Black men and Black women who have been added to the horrifyingly long list of other women, men, and children killed throughout history because of the color of their skin, decimated because of racial and social injustice. Our Asian American brothers and sisters have also experienced untold hate crimes this year, as racist narratives surrounding the virus have been weaponized against them.[1]

Evil against *any people group* has to be named if it's going to be thwarted. So we say the names of those who have been destroyed.

We cry out. Because what cannot be named cannot be repented from or healed.

How will future generations tell the story of 2020? I wonder.

Some have a general sense from the Spirit about what God is doing, but none of us have the full advantage of hindsight yet. Many feel that God is stripping the church of its idols, its showmanship, and its power imbalances. God does seem to be cleaning house, bringing sin and abuse out of the shadows so he can deal with it. Some wonder if this is the actual apocalypse. A friend of mine shrugged her shoulders and said, "I don't know. Nations rise and fall all the time. Maybe this is our moment."

In all the questions and chaos, strange impulses awaken. Wild animals begin to find their way back to the domesticated world without as much human activity happening there. A new species of hornet arrives. Someone told me that the firefly population is at an all-time high. Another person spotted a particular wolverine on a beach shore, one of the thirty left in the world.[2]

God is clearly saying something in the thrum. *But what?*

So I'm doing what I know to do in my questions—trek through this wilderness toward my honeycomb to ask God to drizzle sweetness over my concerns, over the world's concerns.

When at last I arrive, I sit down on my little bench and chug massive gulps from my water bottle. I readjust my sweaty ponytail, pulling the loose hair off my neck, then close my eyes and turn my face toward the sun, dumping all my questions before God.

What the heck is going on, God? Are you still the God of Noah? Is this an ark season? Are you still the God of Cain and Abel? Is this the year we finally learn to take better care of our brothers and sisters? Are you still the God of Abigail? Are you giving us wisdom to stand in the gap when others are foolish? Are you still the God of Paul, sending us to risk life and limb for your gospel? God, who are you in this, our global wilderness? I am so confused, sad, lost. The whole world is. Can you find us here? Can we find you?

Then I stop and breathe deeply, reframing my posture.

"God, my help comes from you," I whisper. "Show me whatever you want to."

After I sit quietly for a time, *this is the place where God shows up.*

Hello, My Name Is God

I was recently invited to cohost a podcast called *Nothing Is Wasted*. We share stories of God's presence in suffering, and I am immensely proud to be a part of this ministry. In every story—a drug overdose, a loved one's unexpected death, a child's health crisis, a spouse's betrayal, a racial trauma—every single person interviewed says some version of "I don't know how to explain it, but in my wilderness, God found me."

This is the place where God shows up is what they are saying.

When Moses was isolated on the far side of the desert, running from his own tragedy, God showed up and said, *I see you.* When Hagar ran from Sarah and Abraham to her own wasteland, God showed up and Hagar said, *you see me.*

We serve a God who knows the wastelands we are in. Sometimes the wasteland is of our own making, and sometimes it's because of a sweeping trauma we could have never foreseen. In it all, God always finds us. God always shows up.

If we look a little closer at Moses and Hagar's stories, we actually find some incredible similarities in their interactions with God, some patterns that become helpful for us to remember in our own deserts of "lostness" and spiritual drought.

God	Hagar (Genesis 16, 21)	Moses (Exodus 2–4)
sees	ran away from home	ran away from home
pursues	in the desert wilderness	in the desert wilderness
shows up	met God through an angel	met God in the burning bush
speaks	the angel spoke: "Return home" (Genesis 16:9, author's paraphrase).	God spoke: "Return home" (Exodus 3:10, author's paraphrase).
gives purpose	"I will give you more descendants than you can count" (Genesis 16:10, NLT).	"I will save my people through you" (Exodus 3:9-10, author's paraphrase).
is named / names himself	named God *El Roi*, the God who sees	God names himself *I Am.*
hears and responds	Raised Ishmael in the wilderness with the comfort and provision of God. "God was *with* the boy" (Genesis 21:20, emphasis added).	Partnered with God to rescue the people. "I [God] will be with you" (Exodus 3:12).
sets free the enslaved	While living in the Desert of Paran (in Egypt), Hagar found an Egyptian wife for Ishmael. In these ways, Hagar returned to her Egyptian roots. Though she was abandoned by Abraham and Sarah, she was ultimately set free by God and provided for by God.	Returned to his Egyptian home. Partnered with God to set the enslaved Hebrews free and experienced God's miraculous provision.

Here is what we discover when we look at these two stories side by side: In their lowest moments, when they were the most lost they could be, God saw Hagar and Moses, pursued them, revealed himself to them, spoke to them, and gave them a new purpose.

The same is true for you and me. In our wasteland seasons, we are invited to "put on [our] new nature, created to be like God— truly righteous and holy" (Ephesians 4:24, NLT). In our deserts, God sees us. God pursues us. God shows up for us. God speaks to us. God gives us new purpose. God reveals something true about his name and nature. God hears and responds to our needs. In our wastelands, God sets us—and others through us—free.

A "found" object is something that was once discarded but has been picked up, restored, and repurposed with new vision. If you are in a wasteland or wilderness season, God has not forgotten you. As Lisa Bevere says, "God's pursuit *is greater than* your ability to wander."[3]

"God's love for us," writes Dr. Beth Felker Jones, "is not some idealized longing for a sanitized, universal ideal of humanity. It is real love for real people. . . . God's love is big enough to love specifics."[4] God is uninterested in allowing you to have some vague or sterile understanding about yourself or about him. Instead, he reaches into our real, particular, peculiar situations—wherever we are—and finds us so that he can transform us with his love, his true nature, and his calling on our lives.

There's a little conversation that God and Moses have together, a bit later in their journey (Exodus 4:1-5). In it, Moses pleads to God, "What if the Israelites won't believe that you sent me to rescue them?"

God answers Moses' question with a surprising one, "What is that in your hand?"

Moses looks down at what he is holding. "A shepherd's staff," he replies.

The tool that Moses used during his desert days as a shepherd was about to be repurposed for the mission of shepherding God's people from slavery to freedom.

What is in your hands?

There are times when we feel forgotten or overlooked, like we may never escape from our wildernesses or make it through these long, hard days. Rest assured. Your desert instrument will become a divine implement.

Your name is not Lost. *You* are not lost. Like that shepherd's staff, and like Moses and Hagar, you are Found, for eternal glory.

God Is Bigger

God, my help comes from you. Show me whatever you want to.

Back in my own wilderness, I sit on my arboretum bench for a while, then stand up to stretch my legs. As I do, I sense God telling me to walk out into the middle of the prairie grass field in front of me.

I feel totally ridiculous doing this, by the way. But I take a risk and walk out into the very middle of the field. I spot a family of butterflies dancing and darting around in one area and sense that I should stop there. Then, I feel God telling me to turn around, so again, reluctantly, I obey.

Immediately, I notice something come into focus. My honeycomb canopy now forty or so feet away seems so small, so tiny. My eyes take it in—the wooden canopy, dwarfed by the large sky behind it, the luscious white clouds, the vast forest of trees, the sheer capacity of creation in that one tiny corner of the world.

In one big rush, I hear God saying, *Aubrey, you've confined me to this spot, this tiny bench. But I have the entire world in my hands. You're keeping me small, but I am bigger than you could imagine.*

I used to have this reoccurring dream where I crawled through a closed-in maze, a dark one filled with dead leaves, dying vines, and decaying people. I felt trapped and terrified. But then a minuscule amount of light began to break in from a tiny opening in the maze's ceiling. When that happened, I also heard a voice say, *This is how you are letting me love you*. With that, the maze's ceiling flew open, and the entire space became engulfed in light. All the dead things sprang beautifully to life. *But this is how I want to love you*, the voice would declare.

Today, in this field, God is reminding me what he showed me in my dreams then. I tend to keep God too small, too confined, too domesticated, too tame. But God's glory and God's love are ever increasing, ever scandalizing, ever astounding, ever breaking out of our tightly sealed containers.

Even in the scariest of pandemics, even in the face of the worst injustice and evil, even when we are far from him in the loneliest of places, this is the God who sees, the God who pursues, the God who shows up, the God who repurposes, the God who finds us in our small corners of the world, while holding the entire world in his hands.

PART III

HOW IT CHANGES EVERYTHING

Participation in Christ means
abandoning our pretenses, openly
acknowledging our identities as sinners
in bondage, and in the same moment
realizing with a stab of piercing joy that
the victory is already ours in Christ,
won by him who died to save us.

FLEMING RUTLEDGE

THE GOODNESS OF OUR NAMES and our image-bearing potential are not for us alone. When we live in the confidence and flourishing of our true identity, we can't help but scatter that goodness to the people around us. We get to participate with Christ in carrying the goodness of *his* name out into the world.

We are here, alive, on this planet, not for our own name's sake but for the name and renown of One greater. God has an overarching goal for your life, an endgame: for you to know him intimately and make him known to others. As we hold onto our identity in him no matter the situation or season, God shapes us into greater Christlikeness for his Kingdom purposes.

Our names matter deeply to God. But all the names God has for us point us toward the one name that matters above all others; a name that has no match or equal; a name that removes our sins, changes our identities, and gives us victory.

There is only one name worth bowing before, a name with the power to transform us and the world around us.

The name of Jesus.

11

YOU ARE THE CURRENCY
OF THE KINGDOM

Made for God's Purposes

When they handed [a Roman coin] to [Jesus], he asked,
"Whose picture and title are stamped on it?"
  "Caesar's," they replied.
  "Well, then," Jesus said, "give to Caesar what belongs to
Caesar, and give to God what belongs to God."
  His reply completely amazed them.

MARK 12:16-17, NLT

As his beloved, his child, his unveiled, his living statue,
his image and likeness bearer, his found one, you are a
"coin" in God's Kingdom—not a coin to be used, spent,
or discarded, but a treasured coin, a restored coin, a coin
impressed with the image of Jesus.

You are the currency of the Kingdom.

WE'RE IN THE BACKYARD ON AN EARLY FALL EVENING. The boys are roast-
ing marshmallows in our firepit, and Kevin and I are sitting on
collapsible camping chairs near the fire, reflecting back on our
summer and looking ahead to the next few months. We're in a bit
of a conflict—nothing major—but together we're asking God to
show us what the future holds . . . and unfortunately coming to
different conclusions (as we do).

We planted and began leading a church together in 2015, a year I got very sick, a year I lost my cousin tragically, a year our son struggled with health issues. Since that time, much has changed. But due to the COVID-19 pandemic, our boys now have to stay home for online school. We also have one son with special learning needs, and all of this means that an adult has to stay home.

We've debated hiring said adult, but with most of my work accomplishable at home and our tight family budget, it's starting to make sense that if one of us has to step away from church leadership for a time, it should likely be me. We also realize that not all families have this luxury, so perhaps we should see it as a gift. I loved my years as a stay-at-home mom, and this is a rare opportunity to pour additional hours into my children again like I did in those early stages. But also, those were exhausting years when I felt like my calling outside of the home would never come to fruition. And so I am torn.

I've been praying to become more like Jesus, specifically related to his servanthood. So maybe this is God saying, "We're going to take foot washing seriously now, Aubrey."

But something about this conversation pinches me.

In 2015, as I said, I was very sick, confined to a couch for months, physically unable to go up and down the stairs. And I was grieving deeply. My cousin's horrific death was sudden and tragic, a loss we still mourn today. Many of our dreams and plans were put on hold as we entered a period of lament. I wasn't sure we'd ever see our way out. And now, years later, I don't want to go backward. I don't want to get stuck in quicksand again.

I try to explain this to Kevin, carefully, thoughtfully. As he listens he stands up to add more kindling to the fire, stoking it a bit. When I'm finished talking, he considers something for a moment before sitting back down next to me. He grabs my hand,

"I'm going to say something," and, sensing I might ruffle against it, proceeds cautiously. "Just let me say it all before you respond."

I nod for him to continue.

"Sometimes it feels like you're still living in . . . no, that's not it." He stops himself for a moment, then tries again. "Sometimes it's like you're still waging war with 2015. Do you think it's time to embrace a new day, Aubs? I mean, maybe this decision right now doesn't have to be connected to the past. Maybe it's something different."

Easy for you to say, I think, but I choose not to say it out loud. I don't want to hear him, and usually that's my cue—there's some truth in what he's saying. I've been living in the past, as I am wont to do. If I'm not vigilant about my thought life, I tend to get stuck emotionally—in love with ghosts, rehashing old conversations, longing for a past (and sometimes a future), real or imagined.

After we've eaten all the s'mores and the boys are in bed, I put on my pajamas and brush my teeth, thinking about a painting by Jewish artist Arthur Sussman—his beautiful rendering of Jacob wrestling with God. Sussman's portrayal of the biblical name-change story is bloody, disturbing, and filled with swirling, entangled, disembodied body parts, bird feathers, fish scales, men, and angels.[1] If you stare long enough at the chaos, however, you begin to notice something: Patches of light and hope comingle with the turmoil.

As I climb into bed, yanking the bedcovers over me, that painting and a prayer roll through my mind: *God, I've looked backward long enough. I've wrestled with my past and my pain long enough. I want to look ahead now. What is your invitation for me, what is your name for me, in this new season?*

I fall asleep fitfully that night. But the next morning, in that liminal space between waking and dreaming, I hear an inkling of a whisper: *Psalm 23.*

I don't have to look it up to recite its illustrious first line: "The LORD is my shepherd; I have all that I need" (NLT). Today, I translate it slightly: *The Lord is my shepherd; I won't go backward.*

Coin Minting

I wonder about you, friend. Do you feel like you are going backward instead of forward? Are you wrestling to know your calling, your purpose, or your name in your current life phase? Does it seem like you are being hidden? Do the demands on you require much more than you have to give? Does it feel like the dream God placed in your heart will never come to fruition? Are you about ready to give up?

(Please don't give up. We need you.)

If I am being honest, part of my struggle in what feels like any "backward interval" is that I tend to confuse my name with God's. What I mean by that is I often find myself wanting *my* way and *my* will above any other's way or will. I want to be the focus of my own plans and dreams. There, I said it.

But in each new stage of life, the Holy Spirit gracefully invites us away from our own self-focus and toward a life that looks a little bit more like Jesus. That is God's big goal for your life, after all: you, more like Jesus.

So whenever I get this way, trapped and tripped up by my longing to be more or better or different, or whatever swirl of striving I get stuck in, I try to remind myself of a conversation that Jesus once had, a dialogue with some Pharisees about coins (that really wasn't about coins at all):

> Later the leaders sent some Pharisees and supporters of
> Herod to trap Jesus into saying something for which he

could be arrested. "Teacher," they said, "we know how honest you are. You are impartial and don't play favorites. You teach the way of God truthfully. Now tell us—is it right to pay taxes to Caesar or not? Should we pay them, or shouldn't we?"

Jesus saw through their hypocrisy and said, "Why are you trying to trap me? Show me a Roman coin, and I'll tell you." When they handed it to him, he asked, "Whose picture and title are stamped on it?"

"Caesar's," they replied.

"Well, then," Jesus said, "give to Caesar what belongs to Caesar, and give to God what belongs to God."

His reply completely amazed them.

MARK 12:13-17, NLT

When I consider Jesus' words—"Give to Caesar what is Caesar's and to God what is God's"—I understand him to mean that, as his image bearers, we belong to God, not to ourselves, and certainly not to any empire. When I am tempted to become the center of my own destiny, I have to remember whose image I bear, whose name I wear.

You and I are here to bear witness to, shine a light on, and bring glory to one name alone, the name of Jesus. We are here for his Kingdom, not our own castles. Whatever our season looks like, the measure of success is not what we might think of as "successful." As his beloved, his child, his unveiled, his living statue, his image and likeness bearer, his found one, you are a "coin" in God's Kingdom—not a coin to be used, spent, or discarded, but a treasured coin, a restored coin, a coin impressed with the image of Jesus.

You are the currency of the Kingdom.

Of course, we get confused, frail and forgetful humans that we are, thinking we belong to another kingdom—an empire of striving and comparison and hustle, of achievement and power. That can be particularly hard when life feels stagnant or difficult, when we want to do everything we can to *be* something and *make* something of ourselves. Or sometimes even when we're in a growing season of flourishing, we still believe we have to professionalize our callings or do something extraordinary in order to matter in this world. But that's a false name. That's the god of this age blinding us to the glory of God in Jesus Christ (2 Corinthians 4:4).

Author Jen Wilkin writes about what it actually looks like to be image-bearing "coins"[2]:

> Because of the fall, you and I are heavily circulated,
> dinged-up, base-metal fodder for the parking meter. But
> we still bear the image of our God, if only faintly. When
> we joyfully embrace the call to be holy as he is holy, those
> worn-down contours of his likeness begin to be restored
> to sharpness. The divots and scratches inflicted by the
> fall and by our own folly begin to be erased. As we grow
> in holiness, love, goodness, justice, mercy, grace, faith,
> patience, truth, and wisdom, we look increasingly like
> Christ, who looks exactly like God.[3]

You are not called to be noteworthy or special or more successful than your peers, or to be more successful than an earlier version of yourself, or to hustle your way into a better life. You are called to look more like Jesus in each new season. That's what it means to move forward even when the objective measures of life feel like they're going backward.

What you do for Jesus, in each and every new life circumstance, may not even be noticed by many. But God will notice. He will bless you for serving him faithfully in every life phase. You have been called with a great calling, a high calling, a holy calling. In your corner of the world, you are tasked and asked to represent God—to shine brightly with the image and inscription that he has impressed into your soul.

True Greatness

The American poet Jack Gilbert was the winner of all kinds of awards and accolades. He was featured on several magazine covers and had access to the perks that go along with a certain amount of celebrity.

Then he intentionally allowed his name to be forgotten.[4]

Gilbert was deeply uninterested in making a name for himself. Why? Because he preferred a life of wonder and delight, and for him, the two—the celebrity-status life and the wonder-delight life—could not coexist.

This is the lesson, it seems, God is teaching me while I once again find myself at home with my boys: Invisibility is not the same as insignificance.[5] A cruciform existence, a life spent serving others, is a life being developed into one of worship and wonder and gladness.

So, during this interval, I have handed my tasks and title over to someone else on our church staff, and God has given me the grace to do so. (And trust me, I recognize the irony that a role at a church *is* a servant's role; it's not a "title." Still, it's been a struggle to let go.)

It's not forever, I know. And I am doing my best to joyfully embrace this time at home. I trust that God is using this circumstance, as he does in all our circumstances when surrendered to him, to make me more like that polished coin he created me to be.

I am also learning to internalize what Beth Moore says,

> True greatness will never come to those who seek to be great. It will come to those who make themselves of no reputation and give their unseen everyday lives, their everyday energies, their everyday faith to serving others amid their own everyday sufferings & unrequited desires.[6]

Maybe you're at home changing diapers and raising littles, wondering if the next season will ever come. Maybe you're embarking on a new career path or earning a new degree, hoping it leads to the next big thing. Maybe you are heading up a new project or organization. Or maybe God has put you on the sidelines for a time.

At the end of the day, the things we achieve, the positions we lead, are not as important as the One we serve. Any role, any title, any leadership successes—they are beautiful things, gifts from God, but they are secondary things when compared to the joy of being made like Jesus and making him known.

In all of it, through every new juncture, you are called to reflect Jesus like the image-bearing, name-of-God-wearing coin you are. Each life stage matters for our spiritual formation and growth. Each builds upon the next, in miraculous, transformative ways. So don't despise your life season. And don't give up, either. Reflect God's image in every life phase and watch how he works all things for your good and his glory. How true it is—*if the Lord is your shepherd; you may sometimes fail forward, but you certainly won't go backward. You'll have everything you need.*

12

YOU ARE A NAME GIVER

Ruling, Blessing, and Naming

You are a chosen people. You are royal priests, a holy nation, God's very own possession. As a result, you can show others the goodness of God, for he called you out of the darkness into his wonderful light.

> "Once you had no identity as a people;
>   now you are God's people.
> Once you received no mercy;
>   now you have received God's mercy."

1 PETER 2:9-10, NLT

As God's royal priest, you are invited to follow in Melchizedek's footsteps and Jesus' own footsteps. You are tasked with mediating God's presence—through blessing others by naming them well.

"MOM, LET ME PUT MY T-SHIRT ON FIRST."

My ten-year-old son is wearing giant, goofy-looking goggles as he swims at my parents' neighborhood pool. I'm sitting on a lounge chair, getting some sun, and I want to snap a picture of him because he looks hilarious with his massive bug eyes and wet hair sticking out all over. I know this stage won't last much longer. My oldest son was just in it, and now he's fully a teenager, too self-conscious, too concerned about the opinions of others, to wear a pair of goofy goggles. I want to capture this moment because it's innocent and fleeting.

When my sons were small, older mamas often told me that time would go fast. "They grow up so quickly," they'd say, usually with a tone of foreboding. "Enjoy it while it lasts."

They meant well, of course. But as a young mom, overwhelmed with exhaustion, leaky breasts, spit-up, and diapers, that admonition always annoyed me. *Good*, I'd think. *I hope they grow up quickly.*

Now? I understand their urgency. I now hear in my own voice that same small echo of sadness. It does go fast. The baby who once fit between the crook of your elbow and your wrist—well, his shoes quickly become bigger than yours.

All that to say, I basically threaten my son to take a break from swimming for just a moment so I can take a few pics and mark this moment.

But it's already started, his transition from big kid to teenager. He wants to put on a T-shirt before I take his picture. He's crossing that threshold into self-consciousness, and this mama bear wants to protect her cub from the little snakes of insecurity that will slither in over the next few years. But what life goes unscathed by this particular rite of passage?

Genesis 2 tells the story of Adam's first day on the job. He was tasked to name each animal as they paraded in front of him—lion and lioness, buck and doe, rooster and hen—and as he did, he realized that his match was missing. When Adam saw Eve, his polar partner, his equal, he couldn't help but name her: "Bone of my bones! Flesh of my flesh!" (This was Adam's version of running laps in church, waving his hanky around.)

This story always makes me think of my sons when they were little. They could barely eke out full sentences, but like most little children with fully alive imaginations, they would instinctively name their beloved stuffed animals or special blankets. They seemed to pull these names out of thin air; a beloved brown teddy bear was suddenly dubbed Dr. Dawson, a blue dog unexpectedly named Humphrey. As a young mom, I marveled at my sons' Adam-like capacity to name what they loved. I wonder if God wondered, the same way I did with my own children, at Adam's creativity in naming.

When it came to naming our three sons, like many parents do, Kevin and I put our kids' names through the wringer. We debated, waited, argued, and tested as we did the very personal, prayerful, and pensive work of naming, always running through a list of potential evil nicknames or bad associations, immediately rejecting any names that had either—until we finally united in agreement. We named each of our sons for a prophet, king, and priest, consecutively.

On their birthdays, we sit around the dinner table, reviewing their names. *Do you know why we named you? For whom? And why that specific person?* With each of their namesakes, we gave our boys a model to strive toward. But more important than any of that, as Adam did with Eve, we named our boys from a place of unmitigated love.

Even though my children have been aptly named, I constantly speak other names over them, especially in those sweet moments at bedtime. I actually used to make them hold out their hands and I would tap each finger with a name. Thumb: You are Handsome. Pointer finger: You are Brave. Middle finger: You are Loved by God and by your dad and me. Ring finger: The Holy Spirit is in you. Pinkie: You are a Lion, and so forth—a Warrior, a Kind Soul, a Good Brother, a Good Son, a Peace Maker, a Justice Bringer.[1] Sometimes they'll walk up to me and give me their outstretched hands, wanting to be named again. My youngest will even strip off his socks, wiggle his toes, and ask me to name those as well. (Once, he wanted both of his ears named.)

And in this moment by the pool, I want to speak something else over my boy. I want to say, "Why are you putting your shirt on, buddy? Your belly is great! Show it off for the world to see."

But I keep my mouth shut because that's likely my issue, not his. I'm probably projecting. So I just laugh, tell him how hilarious he is, and snap as many pictures as he'll let me until he grows impatient to jump back in the pool.

I used to think that the act of naming was part of what made us human, part of our special dignity and design as image bearers. But naming something or someone is actually not that special. I mean, even Koko the gorilla, famous for her use of American Sign Language, named her kittens and her stuffed animals.

It's not the act of naming alone that matters. It's the *way we name* that counts.

Priesthood of Namers

There has been a pendulum swing for some while, culturally, that says *who you are matters more than what you do*. But both our doing and our being matter deeply to God, and they are inextricably intertwined. In fact, our *doing* should flow from our *being*. As John F. Kilner suggests, "God intends images of God to reflect distinctive particulars of what God is *and* does."[2] Both our ontology (our being) and our functionality (our doing) are important.

If we look at the instructions God gave to Adam and Eve in Genesis, what we sometimes refer to as "the cultural mandate"— "Be fruitful and increase in number; fill the earth and subdue it. Rule over the fish in the sea and the birds in the sky and over every living creature that moves on the ground" (Genesis 1:28)—we see that we are meant to reign, govern, and create a life-giving world where others can flourish, but in a very specific way. Not as bosses, not as lords, not as oppressors. But as cultivators and stewards who make famous the name of the Creator.

From the beginning of time, the presence of God was always intended to be revealed and intermediated through humanity. This is why God ignited Adam and Eve to fill the earth and subdue it. It's not so they'd have a lot of kids. It's not so they'd have a lot of power. They were commissioned to rule the earth *so that* the entire world would know the presence, power, and mission of God.

As we fulfill God's cultural mandate, we are called to manifest and mediate the presence of God to the world around us. And through a series of names in 1 Peter 2:9, we discover exactly how we do that:

> You are a chosen people. You are royal priests, a holy nation, God's very own possession. As a result, you can show others the goodness of God, for he called you out of the darkness into his wonderful light.
>
> "Once you had no identity as a people;
>   now you are God's people.
> Once you received no mercy;
>   now you have received God's mercy."
>
> 1 PETER 2:9-10, NLT

According to this passage, you are:

- Chosen
- Royal

- A Priest
- A Holy Nation
- God's Special Possession
- Out of Darkness
- In Wonderful Light
- God's People
- Recipient of Mercy

These God-given names are not for you or me to simply hold close and keep to ourselves. These names are far bigger than that: They are a God-given calling to show others the goodness of God (1 Peter 2:9).

That is what it means to be a royal priest.

In the Order of Melchizedek

What does it mean to be a royal priest? We get a glimpse of the answer in a short story in Scripture about a mysterious (but central) figure, the kingly priest Melchizedek. His name means "king of righteousness," and he ruled over a city named Salem, or "shalom."

Melchizedek appears on the biblical scene just after Abraham defeated some enemies in Sodom. Abraham gathered with a few other kings to bring a sort of ceremonial conclusion to the conflict. At this gathering, the royal priest Melchizedek appears almost inexplicably, acting as a divine mediator.

In just three verses, we find all we need to know about him: "Melchizedek king of Salem brought out bread and wine. He was priest of God Most High, and he blessed Abram, saying, 'Blessed be Abram by God Most High, Creator of heaven and earth. And praise be to God Most High, who delivered your enemies into your hand'" (Genesis 14:18-20).

As a royal priest, Melchizedek does three profound things:

1. He sets out a table of bread and wine
   (among enemies).
2. He praises God.
3. He "names" Abram: *Blessed.*

Later in Scripture, we are told that Jesus is a priest forever in the order of Melchizedek (Psalm 110; Hebrews 7). In other words, Jesus came as the Almighty King of Shalom, the Great High Priest, and the Blessed Namer. And now as God's royal priesthood, you and I are invited to follow in Melchizedek's footsteps and Jesus' own footsteps. We are tasked with mediating God's presence—through blessing others by naming them well.

Each of us, as royal priests, have opportunities in our days and relationships to speak blessed names over the people around us. Here are a few examples to spark your imagination:

- **Becoming Names:** One thing I love about CrossFit (from my limited knowledge of CrossFit culture) is that everyone there is called "athlete." Even if you're new to CrossFit, even if you've never done a pull-up or a tire flip in your ever-loving life, everyone at CrossFit calls you "athlete." Why? Simply because you have been brave enough to show up and do the work. Though you may not feel like, see yourself as, or name yourself "athlete" now, you are on your way to becoming one.[3]

  We can name others by their eschatological (fullness of time) identity, based on who they are becoming. Calling others by their *becoming* names is speaking out the truth of who Jesus says they are now and will be one day.

- **Reimagined False Names:** A friend of Kevin's was wrestling with a new name: "Asperger's." He was recently diagnosed and confided in us, "I hate the word so much. It doesn't necessarily hold me back, but I feel like less of a person now."

  Kevin asked him if he'd ever spent time talking to God about it. He hadn't but was willing to let Kevin pray for him. When Kevin prayed, he asked, "God, what gifts are hidden here in Asperger's that my friend can't see yet? God, he is reacting so strongly to this name; what do you want to show him in it?"

  As they prayed, the Holy Spirit showed them the root of his struggle. "Asperger's" wasn't necessarily the source of his grief; it was the false name underneath: Mistake. Through tears, he confided in Kevin, "Since I was diagnosed, I've been believing a lie—that I am a mistake."

  That day, Kevin asked God to remind his friend of his true name and to eradicate the name "Mistake" from his soul. When they reconnected a few months later, he told Kevin that he was learning to understand Asperger's and appreciate its gifts. "I am learning to embrace myself as I am. More than that, I realize I am not 'Mistake.' That false name is gone. God is helping me embrace a new identity."

  We can help others understand the places where they are believing false identities and discover instead God's beautifully reimagined name for them.

- **Prophetic Names:** Every time we met for a girl's night out, I kept "seeing" the name Healer on my friend's forehead. One day, I finally worked up the courage to tell her, "I know this may sound weird, but I see 'Healer' on your forehead every time we're together."

Tears immediately pooled in her eyes as she told me that she had felt burdened to start an organization for women who've been abused or abandoned, but she hadn't acted on it—out of insecurity. That "name" gave her the affirmation she needed, and she's been running a thriving nonprofit, ministering to hundreds of women, ever since. She recently shared with me that she refers back to this moment whenever the enemy tries to tell her she's not qualified to lead and execute the vision God has given her: "I remind myself of this conversation often, and it helps me push past the lies."[4]

Sometimes God gives us a glimpse of a truth about someone that answers something they've been asking him. We can participate in God's prophetic-naming ministry by offering what he's placed on our hearts about them. We have no idea the eternal impact this will have in their lives and in the lives of others through them.

As God's royal priest, you are meant to, very intentionally, share the love and presence of Jesus with every person you come into contact with—be it a friend, stranger, or enemy—by naming them well.

In a world hell-bent on stripping us of our identity, in a culture that so often pressures us into the trap of comparison, in a sphere that regularly dehumanizes other image bearers—in a society that tears others down all the time—

the act of seeing someone, truly seeing them,

welcoming them,

and blessing them with a dignifying name,

is one powerful way of putting on your royal, priestly robes and getting to work.

Who Am I?

German theologian Jürgen Moltmann, describing the difference between animals and humans, once noted, "A cow is always simply a cow. It does not ask, 'What is a cow? Who am I?' Only man asks such questions and indeed clearly has to ask them about himself and his being. This is his question. His question follows him in hundreds of forms."[5]

Who am I? This is the question my goofy-goggle-wearing son is asking and will keep on asking as he moves into new stages and phases of adolescence.

This is the question the entire world is asking.

You are empowered, in Jesus, to answer.

As my friend, pastor and author, Ashlee Eiland writes, "Let's do the work of living out of our good, true names and using good, true names of one another. Let's call one another Warrior, Survivor, Teacher, Friend, Artist, Advocate, Hero, and Optimist. The world needs more of what's good and true in us. It needs to be reminded that we're miracles."[6]

So name your neighbors, strangers, and enemies with honor. This is your sacred responsibility. Speak dignifying goodness over them and about them. Refuse to tear them down with your words. Set tables before them with a feast of encouragement. This is the way of Jesus, our Great High Priest and Royal Namer.

13

YOU ARE SENT

Living Your Name

Build homes, and plan to stay. Plant gardens, and eat the food
they produce. Marry and have children. Then find spouses for
them so that you may have many grandchildren. Multiply! Do
not dwindle away! And work for the peace and prosperity of
the city where I sent you into exile. Pray to the LORD for it, for
its welfare will determine your welfare.

JEREMIAH 29:5-7, NLT

**God masterfully utilizes all the ways he has named us so
that we can minister to others. . . . You are invited by God
to excavate from your life's narrative, your gift mix, and
your passions—the calling that accompanies your name.**

EVERY SUMMER, I TAKE MY BOYS FISHING. Well, I should clarify. I walk
them down to the dock, helping them juggle their tackle boxes
and fishing rods and life vests so that my dad, *Pops*, can take them
fishing. My oldest has become a fairly skilled fisherman over the
years, but with my littles, it's a pretty entertaining show to watch.
Basically, it goes a little something like this:

Pops helps them put on and zip up their life jackets.

Pops helps the boys fix any fishing line that's tangled or needs
to be replaced.

Pops supplies and also hooks the bait because my boys are too grossed out to pierce slimy worm skin.

Pops kneels (on his bad knees) and wraps his arms around the boys.

Pops shows them how to hold the rod properly.

Pops helps them cast the reel.

Pops models patience, while they get antsy, *dyyyiiiinnnng* for the fish to bite.

Pops offers a little fishing wisdom: "A good fisherman is still; he doesn't scare the fish away. A good fisherman is chill, smooth as the water's glassy surface. A good fisherman uses his will, in order to be patient and quiet. And a good fisherman experiences the thrill of the catch."

If the fish are biting, and if my boys feel that first tug on the line, I watch and laugh because they inevitably panic and let go, nearly releasing the rod into the lake. But Pops is nimble, ready to grab the pole and help the boys reel in the fish. Of course, once the fish is reeled in, the boys are too freaked out to touch the flapping creature, so Pops unhooks it for them and lobs it back into the water with a splash.

When all is said and done, Pops high-fives the boys and exclaims with grandfatherly pride and affection, "Look at what you did! You caught a fish! I am so proud of you!"

Then he names them, "You are such excellent fishermen!"

And though we all know who *really* caught the fish, whose experience, whose equipment, whose wherewithal, whose skill set, whose patience actually claimed the freshwater prize—throughout the rest of the day, Pops makes phone calls and goes on social media and tells strangers in the grocery store about what incredible fishermen his grandsons are.

All of it gives them the courage to try again each summer, until the day they finally grow into the fishermen he has all along been preparing them to become.

God has named you. You are fully known, exquisitely loved, and securely held in his arms. He has given you names out of who you are now and for who you are in the process of becoming. But God doesn't bring you into this knowledge for knowledge's sake alone or even for your personal transformation alone. He doesn't just give you all the information about your identity, doesn't just tell you all the truths about yourself so you can sit there quietly and stare out at the water.

We are named to *go and live out our names*. We are called to live as "sent ones" on God's mission into the world. And the great news is that God himself equips us for the task. It's God's arms around us, God's wisdom guiding us, God's patience preparing us, and God's leading that enables us to live on mission for him.

This is who he has all along been preparing us to become.

Named and Sent

The names you carry will give you courage to move through the world with clarity and purpose for God's name and Kingdom. God has a lot to say about *who* you are and *whose* you are. Your next step? To let it change everything, in how you live and what you do. You are invited to participate in God's work in the world. You have been *named* to go share the name of Jesus.

Maybe you're already living into your name or maybe you're wondering how to even begin. God masterfully utilizes all the ways he has "named" us so that we can minister to others. He has not created you accidentally. You were creatively, imaginatively, and purposefully portioned—designed and destined by God to reflect his goodness to the world around you. And you are invited by

God to excavate from your life's narrative, your gift mix, and your passions—the calling that accompanies your name.

What I mean is: Your *beingness*, your *namedness*, is essential to your *doingness*.

Here are a few questions to ask yourself and your community—your church family, your friends, your inner circle—to help you unearth what to do with the names you've been given:[1]

1. *What am I good at?* God is not going to call you to be a professional basketball player if, like me, you can't manage holding a ball and walking simultaneously. We all have to get out of our areas of comfort, but God will use your strengths as part of your calling. If you struggle to know what your strengths are, ask your community to offer some insight.

2. *What am I passionate about?* Or if "passion" is too much pressure, what sparks your curiosity? What interests you, intrigues you? What do you wake up thinking about? What would you love to pour more time into? God has given you your passions for a divine purpose.

3. *What does my neighborhood, city, school, and/or world need?*[2] What wrongs can you work to make right? What injustices or disadvantages anger you that you want to fix? Perhaps you and your community are the ones to help make a difference.

4. *"What are the open doors in [my] life?"*[3] Don't waste your life banging on closed doors. Ask God to show you what paths and purposes he is anointing in your life. And along with that, don't worry so much about the doors God is opening

for other people. He's got them on their own journey, just as he has you on yours.

5. *What season of life am I in?* A college student, a stay-at-home parent, and a marketplace employee are in three totally different life seasons. That's not a mistake. God uses each season to shape us and ready us for the next phase of our callings. Don't despise any life season, for the Lord rejoices in small beginnings (Zechariah 4:10).

6. *What is my personality type and gift mix?* God uses the specific ways he has made you and named you to help you understand what you have been put on this earth to do. Self-assessment tools (Enneagram, CliftonStrengths, APEST, Myers-Briggs, or others like them) are a useful way to help you get to know yourself and, therefore, your calling.

7. *What does my Christian community sense God calling us to do?* Calling or sentness isn't always an individual pursuit. What is God calling your church community to do? What group of people is God calling your squad to minister to?

8. *What does a "timeline" of my life reveal?* Draw a timeline of your life, with all your big life experiences in chronological order. Step back and notice any themes, any patterns, any processes that God has used in your life. What names have defined your life trajectory? Ask God to reveal to you what your life story might mean for what he's calling you to do.

The prophet Jeremiah called God's people to pray for and work toward the peace and prosperity of the city, to "build homes, and plan to stay. Plant gardens, and eat the food they produce. Marry and have children. Then find spouses for them so that you may have many grandchildren. Multiply! Do not dwindle away!" (Jeremiah 29:5-6, NLT).

You are invited to participate with God in making your world into a garden-like, shalom-like place where others are empowered to flourish. This has been your mandate since the Garden of Eden. You are here to work for the prosperity and peace of wherever God has you. (Basically, if your dreams are all about you, you aren't dreaming big enough yet.)

You have been named to do something—for God's glory and Jesus' name. This might not end up being your career, but whatever your career or season of life is, this is what you are called to do for the Kingdom. God takes the raw material of our personalities, our experiences, our Christian community, and the Spirit's work in our lives to craft our sentness.

God has named you with perfect plans to send you.

Stay Faithful

This might go without saying, but I *have* to say it here—far too many Christian leaders, in their pursuit of calling, their *sentness*, and their own names, have led secret lives. It's a devastating thing, time and time again, to discover that our earthly heroes have chosen lives of moral failure, secret sin, or worse, that all along they have been perverse, exploitative predators. We have seen a lot of wolves in sheep's clothing over the years.

If you want to live out your *namedness* for God, if you want to run after your calling, if you want to change the world, do you know what matters deeply? Your character.

Not your talent, not your achievements, not your charisma, not your intelligence, not your beauty, not your skill set, but your inner and outer life looking *and* becoming like Jesus.

This doesn't mean perfection, but it certainly means faithfulness. And it definitely means integrity.

Run the race. Stay faithful. Be the same on the inside as you are on the outside (Psalm 101). *That*, my friend, is world-changing. *That* is garden-making. *That* is biblical sentness. *That* is living into your name. *That* is learning to "catch fish" as you partner with God.

Speaking of which, a few years ago, my oldest son was featured in a fishing magazine in a little section on young fisherman.[4] They published a picture of him and Kevin fishing for sheepshead and bull redfish off the coast of Florida and mentioned his dream of one day catching a dorado.

Because Pops invited him, because Pops equipped him, because Pops showed persistent patience, because Pops wrapped his arms around him, because Pops empowered him—our son has known the joy, delight, and satisfaction of the catch.

Sentness flows from mature character and integrity, formed in the graduate school of life.[5] Over your lifetime, as you experience encounters with God's Word, God's power, God's patience, God's equipping, God's wisdom, God's Spirit in you, and God's arms around you—you are being shaped to become the excellent fisher of people that he has named and sent you to be.

14

HE IS THE NAME ABOVE EVERY OTHER

The Name of Jesus

Christ is the visible image of the invisible God.
He existed before anything was created and is
supreme over all creation.

COLOSSIANS 1:15, NLT

Most names are a proclamation or a statement of identity.

Jesus' name is the only name that *does* something.

"LORD, WE'RE HERE FOR YOU and ready to listen to your voice."

I am standing up behind a table in a classroom filled with peers and schoolmates. We have our eyes closed and our "spiritual ears" open, trying to hear from God. We've specifically asked God about next steps. *What do you want us to do next, God, in our families, in our studies, in our home, in our places of work?*

In this class we've spent a lot of time learning ancient spiritual practices and biblical methods of being with God, and now we are transitioning a bit to doing. *Out of all we know about who we are, and who God has called us to be, out of our rest in God, what then should we do? How then should we live?*

We crazy Christians have the audacity to think we can actually hear from God. But I'm kind of struggling internally in this moment, because for some reason God doesn't seem to be speaking to me.

Meanwhile my classmates totally get into this exercise. I'm listening to them utter phrases like, "Thank you, God." Or, "Yes I hear you, Lord." Or they're crying, clearly touched by God's presence, his perfectly personal answer to their questions.

And I'm over here like HELLLOOOOO? GOD? YA THERE? I actually start to weigh how unethical it would be to pretend like I am hearing from God. Can I just throw out a "Yes, Lord, you're comin' in loud and clear," for my professor's and friends' sake?

But then, of course, I do hear God's faithful still, small voice. So I join in the chorus of my classmates saying "Thank you, Lord," and I mean it.

How easily I forget that this is an actual miracle: The God who breathed the world into existence, the God who knows every piece of who we are, also wants to be known and heard by us. What a gift. What a grace. What a thing.

God brings to mind some Scripture that I had been reading earlier that morning: the reconciliatory moment between Jesus and Peter, when Jesus asked his friend that triplicate question, "Do you love me? Do you love me? Do you love me? . . . You do? Well then, feed my sheep."

I hear God saying something similar now, "Aubrey, feed my sheep," along with an additional phrase: "Don't fill your stadium."

Now, I'm not over here filling stadiums, not even close—most of us aren't. We're just trying to make ends meet, attempting to make sure our friends and families are loved and safe, and hoping to make a little bit of meaning from our lives.

But what God is saying to me when he says, "Feed my sheep; don't fill your stadium" is this: *Who you are and the names you carry aren't here for your name's sake. You don't exist for your own glory or "fame." You are here to serve and bow down to one name: the name of Jesus.*

What Does the Name of Jesus Do?

The book of Colossians declares boldly, defiantly, that Jesus is the visible image of the invisible God (1:15). Because humanity did not bear God's image as we were meant to, Jesus came as the definitive and decisive *imago*. Jesus shows us what God is like and how we can be more like God. And perhaps most importantly, Jesus *makes this happen*.

Because of his loving sacrifice, his blood, his stripes, his resurrection power, and his name, sinful humans are able to bear God's image and wear the names God has for us as we were always intended to. And Jesus did all of this by living into his own name: *Immanuel*, God with us.

Jesus, who is fully God, became fully human so that humanity could be fully restored. In Jesus, the medium was the message; Jesus—as totally human and totally divine with no division, separation, confusion, or change—makes the way and *is the way* for us to be reconciled to a divine God.

In Jesus, we find the one name, the true name, the exalted-above-every-other name, the name that holds all things together, the name that has no beginning and no end, and the name that *is* the beginning and the end. While most names are a proclamation or a statement of identity, Jesus' name is the only name that *does* something—a lot of somethings.

- In the name of Jesus, the principalities and powers of evil were demolished, and death was destroyed (Psalm 110:1; Hebrews 2:4-15; 1 John 3:8).

- In the name of Jesus, the sinless, spotless Lamb of God, the penalty and punishment that brought us peace was placed on him, and "by his wounds we are healed" (Isaiah 53:5).

- In the name of Jesus, we were ransomed (Mark 10:45).

- In the name of Jesus, sin is forgiven (Luke 7:47-48).

- In the name of Jesus, we have life (John 20:31).

- In the name of Jesus, just as we were all involved in Adam's sin and its appalling consequences, so we all participate in Jesus' death and triumph (Romans 5:12-21).

- In the name of Jesus, we are made new and reconciled to God, and we become ministers of reconciliation ourselves (2 Corinthians 5:17-21).

- In the name of Jesus, we are united with God through the Spirit and able to live like him and have his mindset (Philippians 2:1-5).

- In the name of Jesus, every knee will bow down and every tongue will confess that he, alone, is Lord (Philippians 2:9-11).

- In the name of Jesus, we are made holy, participants in the divine life (1 Peter 1:16).

- In the name of Jesus, the love of God as seen on the cross moves us to love God and love others (1 John 4:7-10).

- In the name of Jesus, all things are being made new (Revelation 21:5).

Do you see the shockingly massive work of Jesus' name for you and for the world? Jesus paid the price. Jesus took your place. Jesus destroyed death. Jesus conquered Satan. Jesus sets you free from the personal and cosmic powers of sin. Jesus gives you life and shows you how to live. Jesus is making all things new. What a salvation! What a name! In the words of American philosopher and orthodox theologian David Bentley Hart,

> When all is said and done . . . we are to be guided by the full character of what is revealed of God in Christ. For, after all, if it is from Christ that we are to learn how God relates himself to sin, suffering, evil, and death, it would seem that he provides us little evidence of anything other than a regal, relentless, and miraculous enmity: sin he forgives, suffering he heals, evil he casts out, and death he conquers.[1]

In the mighty name of Jesus, you have been brought from death to life. In the loving name of Jesus, you live in and under his grace. In the virtuous name of Jesus, you are an instrument of righteousness. In the victorious name of Jesus, you overcome the enemy, death. In the incomparable name of Jesus, you are made, you are loved, you are named, you are known.

Look to Jesus

This is what it means to be fully known: to know Jesus, who turned everything on its head by making himself in *our* image and *our* likeness, coming to earth as a human, wrapping himself in sinless flesh, so that we could find our salvation, our life, and our known-ness in him.

- So when the ground beneath you feels unsteady, look to Jesus.
- When you wonder who you are—look to Jesus.

- When you are threatened with shame about your name, look to Jesus.
- When you feel like you'll never be good enough, look to Jesus.
- When a hero lets you down, look to Jesus.
- When the evil in the world feels too heavy, look to Jesus.
- When you are overwhelmed by pain or suffering, look to Jesus.
- When you feel lost in the monotony of daily life, look to Jesus.
- When you wonder if God can find you in your wilderness, look to Jesus.
- When you don't know if God sees you, look to Jesus.
- When you feel alone, look to Jesus.
- When you question your worth and value, look to Jesus.
- When you feel trapped, look to Jesus.
- When you've failed again, look to Jesus.
- When you need security, look to Jesus.
- When you long for rest, look to Jesus.
- When you need hope, look to Jesus.
- When all seems lost, look to Jesus.
- When you think you are unworthy of love, look to Jesus.
- When your false names speak loudly, look to Jesus.

As we began our journey together, I asked you a question: *What is your name?*

I hope by now the answer is clear.

The only one who has the right to name you is the one who knows you fully and completely, the one who gave up everything for you—Jesus Christ, the one with a name above every other.

———•———

The apostle John ends his book with these words: "The disciples saw Jesus do many other miraculous signs in addition to the ones recorded in this book. But these are written so that you may continue to believe that Jesus is the Messiah, the Son of God, and that by believing in him you will have life by the power of his name" (John 20:30-31, NLT).

In other words, Jesus' name does what no other name can— His name changes everything.

ACKNOWLEDGMENTS

Dear Reader,

If you're considering writing a book in a pandemic, step away from your computer. If you have the opportunity to read a book on a beach, go on an adventurous vacation, or cozy up in some idyllic log-cabin situation, do that instead. So many times while working on this project, I felt so distant from myself, distant from my words, distant from my emotions, distant from what God wanted this book to be. I wasn't sure how to see my way through the pandemic, let alone a book project in the midst of one. (In one rendition, this book had *many* Latin words in it, if that gives you any sense of how I was coping.)

But as God tends to do with the tools in our hands, this project became a respite from so much pain and death and heartache all around. I think with my fingers. I pray with my fingers. I find God with my fingers. And so many times, when I was tempted to despair, God found me, and we wrote together.

So, all in all, this book was borne in the wildest wilderness of our collective existence, and though I would not recommend writing while the world is falling apart, I am deeply grateful. Because of my incredible family, my community, my amazing editor, and you(!), *Known* came together, and it feels like a miracle.

———•———

Kevin, Eli, Lincoln, Nolan—You are the great loves of my life. Thank you for being you. I love you. I like you. I adore you. I am obsessed with your names and the way you live into them.

My parents, Lydia and Larry—Thank you for always being supportive, encouraging, and faithful followers of Jesus. Thank you for taking me camping at Mount Saint Helens all those years ago.

The Sampsons—Thank you for your ongoing love for our little family in the middle of a difficult pandemic year.

Caitlyn Carlson—It's a rare gift to call an editor a friend and vice versa. You're a gift to so many writers, and I can't imagine creating anything without you. Thank you for seeing this through when it felt so muddy. Thank you for your vision and your heart.

Christine Caine—You are the real deal. Not only a leader but a spiritual older sister filled with integrity and endurance for Jesus. I am grateful for your influence in my life and around the globe. Thank you for writing this foreword.

My girls: Hollie, Kathy, Amanda, Tara, and Mika—You inspire me as moms, leaders, friends, and women after God's own heart. I am so grateful to know you and be known by you.

Jenn—I dedicated this book to you because you have been and are still the bravest woman I know.

Propel Women—Thank you for letting me be a little part of the work you do to empower women around the globe. Let's keep going!

Renewal Church—You are the greatest church plant in the world. You pivoted with grace when pivots and grace were asked of you in 2020. Thank you.

Propel cohort—To my sister grad students, it is an honor to learn alongside you. Can you believe we are almost done?!!! We are (hopefully!) going to be DOCTORS one day!

Catherine McNiel—You are the hand I hold when I need a hand to squeeze (while I squeeze other hands) and the angel I run to when vampires are after me. Thank you for being you.

Catherine Fitzgerald—Thank you for your last-hour input. I value you and your voice.

NavPress—Caitlyn Carlson, Dave Zimmerman, Olivia Eldredge, and Elizabeth Schroll: the greatest publishing team in the universe. Seriously, you're more than a publishing house. You're also a family. I am grateful to get to hang my stocking on your mantle.

Don Pape—Thanks for believing in me and in this book.

Tyndale—Robin Bermel, Linda Schmitt, Whitney Harrison, Eva Winters, Madeline Daniels, and the rest of the many, many people at Tyndale who cared for this book. What a beautiful thing it is to see a marriage between organizations with the same vision who want to make disciples and take more ground for Jesus' name through creativity and writing. Thank you for all your work and for this amazing cover, yet again!

Kaitlyn Bouchillon—Thank you for managing this book launch and becoming a new friend in the process. I am so grateful for your creative vision.

Redbud and hope*writers—Thank you for creating safe spaces for writers to grow and express their voices. I can't believe I get to know you.

Nothing is Wasted and *The Common Good* crews—This work is life-giving. Taylor, Davey and Kristi, Tommy, and the whole NIW team, *and* Brian and Debbie at TCG and Marcus, Jeff, and the whole team at AM1160—I am grateful you let me share your headphone space. You're some of my favorite people.

Tawny Johnson and Illuminate Literary—Thanks for believing in this project and in me.

Christina Walker—My spiritual director and guide. I borrowed your faith more times that I can count. Thank you for pouring wisdom, grace, and the voice of God over me. You're a gift to me and so many.

Shannon Ethridge—My first writing mentor. I would not be on my third book without you.

Reader—It's you I write for, you I pray for when I go to sleep, and you I wake up wondering how to encourage each day. May Jesus meet you when you feel unknown, and may you find yourself so deeply known and loved by the God who made you and named you.

Appendix A

GOD'S MANY NAMES

OUR NAMES ONLY HAVE WEIGHT and power because of the One who has named us. We can better discern God's voice and believe his names for us—believe our *known-ness*—when we more fully understand who *he* is. God's names are active, showing us who he is, how he works, and the many different ways we can cry out to him. There are more than a hundred names of God in Scripture, and I encourage you to study them to learn more about this God who names you. Here are a few of the names of God I have personally held on to throughout my life.

El Roi: The God Who Sees Me

Hagar was a slave, a woman who became a pawn in Abraham and Sarah's impatience as they waited for the Lord's plan to unfold. She knew what it was like to be unseen by the people around her. Impregnated by her master, then abused and left alone, Hagar found herself in a desert when an angel appeared, telling her that God had heard her cries and had plans for her and the child in her womb. Immediately, she declared, "You are *El Roi*, the God who sees me." Hagar was one of the first female theologians, one of the first people outside of the Hebrew family to give God a name. And like Hagar—in our moments of feeling abandoned, isolated, and alone—we can call out to *El Roi*, knowing that no matter where we are, our God *sees* us. *(See Genesis 16:1-16.)*

Jehovah Rohi: The Lord Is My Shepherd

In the ancient world, a shepherd served as the provider and protector of the flock, the one who would lead sheep to pasture and water and fight off any attacking wolves. Our God is a shepherd, but not just any shepherd; God is a royal shepherd, ruling over the sheep (us) and reigning over every circumstance. When we need sovereign provision, protection, and leading in our own lives, we can call on *Jehovah Rohi*, the Lord our shepherd. *(See Psalm 23.)*

El Elyon: God Most High

When everything around us is spiraling out of control, we need to remember that God is the Lord above all. When idolatry threatens to overtake our nations, our governments, and our churches, or when we are fixated on our own circumstances and can't seem to break free, we need to cling to the name *El Elyon*, remembering that the Lord who created everything is still in control and remains most high. *(See Genesis 14:18-20; Deuteronomy 26:19; Psalm 57:2.)*

Jehovah Tsidkenu: Our Righteousness

In a world bent on equating righteousness with being a "good person," our daily failures, shortcomings, and sins scream that no amount of willpower can truly make us *good enough*. We need a

Savior, someone to do what our weak flesh cannot. Jesus came so that in those moments when our imperfection threatens to derail us, we can call on *Jehovah Tsidkenu*, the Lord our righteousness. *(See Jeremiah 23:5-6.)*

El Olam: Everlasting God

Often, our finite perspectives get blurred because the moment feels pressing, the unimportant things, the urgent things, can quickly overshadow our perspective about what really matters. Those are the moments in which we need a reminder of a God who has *always been* and will *always be*. We need to cry out to *El Olam*, the Everlasting God. *(See Psalm 90:1-2.)*

Jehovah Nissi: My Banner

Life is full of battles. In our homes, in our workplaces, in our schools, in our churches, in our neighborhoods. Sometimes it feels like there is an all-out war everywhere we turn. We can feel like the underdog, like everything is stacked against us, just like the Israelites as they made their way toward a future of hope. They faced attacks at every bend—yet they never fought alone. With every arrow of attack stacked against us, we need to raise a banner, a symbol of victory in our most gruesome wars, as a reminder that *Jehovah Nissi* never leaves our side. *(See Exodus 17:15.)*

Jehovah Mekaddishkem: The Lord Who Sanctifies

In Christ, we have been set apart, made holy. We continue to live in this world while wrestling with what it means to not be of it. The process of growing in the likeness of Jesus is a lifelong one through sanctification, the daily refinement of our lives to reflect his. It's easy to want to force ourselves to *be better* when the truth is that power to transform us resides with the Lord who sanctifies. When you find yourself trying to force yourself into a cruciform life, ask for *Jehovah Mekaddishkem* to help you. *(See Exodus 31:13; 1 Peter 1:15-16.)*

Jehovah Shalom: The Lord Is Peace

We know what it is like to live in unrest. With wars and threat of wars raging in our world and with the internal battles of fear storming within, finding shalom feels nearly impossible. The Israelites and Gideon knew this same kind of uncertainty and anxiety, as enemies threatened to destroy them. Gideon needed to be reminded that the Lord was with him, even when his army was weaker than its opponents. So God encouraged Gideon—giving him the peace he needed to declare his trust in *Jehovah Shalom*. The same reassurance Gideon received is also ours from the Lord of peace. *(See Judges 6:24.)*

Yahweh Rapha: The Lord Who Heals

As we try whatever means necessary to rid ourselves of pain, we often overlook the reality that God is a healer. Do you remember how Jesus walked into town, spit on the dirt, and slathered the paste on the eyes of a blind man so that he could see once and for all? Healing was a central part of Jesus' ministry, and our unchanging God is still a healer today. With all the brokenness that comes from being a part of this sin-riddled world, whether physical, mental, emotional, or spiritual, we need to remember that God heals. And while healing may come in a way we aren't expecting, *Yahweh Rapha* is always willing to hear our prayers for it. *(See Exodus 15:26; Psalm 103:2-3; Matthew 4:23.)*

Adonai: Lord

There is no name more simple or more powerful that we can call God. *Adonai* simply translates as Lord, communicating his position as it rolls off our tongues. And through it, we remember that he is our master, our authority, our King. And as we fight to build our own kingdoms, declaring "our will be done," no other name rightly puts us in our place quite like this one. For the days you need to remember that it is not *your* kingdom come, but his, call upon the only name that matters: *Adonai. (See Exodus 4:10-11.)*

REFLECTION & DISCUSSION GUIDE

THIS GUIDE CAN BE USED for personal reflection or small-group discussion. Because the topic of names and naming is so important, studying and discussing this book in community will be a powerful experience. In this way, you can invite others to speak into your "name" journey and you can breathe life into theirs.

If you decide to lead a small-group or community book discussion, consider beginning with an icebreaker to make everyone feel comfortable, open and/or close with prayer, and be sure to designate at least one person who will move the discussion forward each week. (That might be you, or it might be a rotating team of discussion leaders.) Namedness can be a vulnerable topic, so you'll also want to make sure that the group keeps things confidential and that everyone feels safe and secure enough to open up.

Should you decide, instead, to walk through this guide for your personal devotion, I still believe God will meet you tenderly and powerfully.

Part I: Who You Are

Name 1. Beloved: Did God Really Say?
Scripture Reading: Genesis 1:28, 31; 3:1; Psalm 116:7; Luke 10:30-37

Beloved. The word itself hides within it the definition: *be loved.* But a lifetime of hurt and disappointment, sometimes from the people who were supposed to show you the most love, can make you wonder if this name is true for you.

We can live our lives striving and working for this name, hoping that tipping the scales by doing good or proving our worth will make us loved once and for all. Or we can look at all the ways we have fallen short and believe that this is a name we can never claim as ours.

Yet, whether we live in striving or in shame, *Beloved is always ours.* God's love for us is unaffected by our overcompensation or our underperformance. His love is ours. Our name is *Beloved.*

QUESTIONS

1. Henri Nouwen said, "Being the Beloved expresses the core truth of our existence." If you were to get to the core of who you are and how you see yourself, would you honestly describe yourself as *Beloved*? What keeps you from feeling as if you are beloved? What helps you to feel it most?

2. Are you tempted to strive to earn God's love? What might this look like?

3. Why is the name *Beloved* so foundational? How can believing the truth of it affect how you move and operate in the world?

4. Adam and Eve were deceived by the question *Did God really say?*, and we are as well. How does Satan ask this question to you in your own life? What are some crafty ways he casts doubt in you over your name *Beloved*? How can you be mindful of that and fight against the schemes of the enemy in the victory of Jesus?

5. One of the reasons we can struggle with accepting that we are *Beloved* is because we have created subconscious definitions of who or what characteristics are deserving of such a name. If you were to be honest, what are some of the traits of someone you think is worthy of being called *Beloved*? How does that compare to who God actually calls *Beloved*?

6. How would a person who understands that their name is *Beloved* live? How would a movement of people resting securely in God's love influence our particular cultural moment?

7. What is one way you could live *Beloved* right now?

Beloved is the name from which all others flow. Knowing and understanding the love God has for *you*—yes *you*—with all your sins and scars and idiosyncrasies has the power to change your life. Learning to internalize this name and receive it as yours is how you can move from striving or hiding and into the resting arms of the Father.

PRAYER PROMPT

Lord, I tend to strive to earn your love or I hide in shame over my past brokenness. Please teach me to live beloved. At the core of who I am, let me rest in your love, knowing it is not by my doing but by yours alone. In your name I pray, amen.

Name 2. *Known: God Names Us Backward*
Scripture Reading: Psalm 139

We live in a generation that wants to be *known*. Go viral or put out the right content and you have the potential for thousands, if not millions, to know your name. And so we invest ourselves in a virtual world in hopes that one day, we will finally be seen. In our smaller orbits, we have found ways to share parts of ourselves, as curated as they may be, with the people we want to know us.

This begs a question: Why do so many of us feel completely *unknown*? In a time where we are more interconnected than ever, why are the rates of loneliness, depression, and anxiety at an all-time high?

To be known is to be loved. And without a deeply rooted sense that we are fully accepted as we are, our society exchanges *being known* for *being seen*. There's a difference. The kind of knowing David describes in Psalm 139 is that of completeness, where every part of who you are is exposed *and* loved.

The truth is, no amount of oversharing or followers or likes can make us fully known. Other people don't have the capacity to see every crevice and cave that lurks in our souls beyond the surface of what we allow them to see. But, *God knows* because he was there before we were even formed. And that is the greatest gift: Even when we feel misunderstood, unseen, or disconnected, we are, and have always been, fully known.

QUESTIONS

1. If you are able to,* think back to your childhood (*if you had trauma in your childhood, only engage in this activity with support and safety). What are some ways you felt God

was actively engaged with you? What are some meaningful experiences in nature or moments of connection with a parent or mentor? What are some memories in which you were physically alone but not truly alone? What were some peak moments of joy? What does that teach you about how God was active in your life all along?

2. How does knowing God knew you *before* you were even formed make you feel? In what ways is that a comfort? What does that reveal in terms of how well he knows you now?

3. Have you ever felt that God had a name for you? What was it? If not, what is a name he might use to describe you?

4. What does it mean to be *known*? How would you describe feeling completely known?

5. In what ways do you see our culture exchanging being *seen* for being *known*? Why is this dangerous? What are some of the potential effects that could have on human souls?

6. Read Psalm 139. Describe some of the ways David shows how well God knows him. Which of these do you need to remind yourself of? Which is most encouraging to you?

Never allow your desire to be known by your Creator to be exchanged for a pursuit of the world's popularity contest. Think back to all the ways in which you have seen God's hand in your life, showing you that even *before* this moment, you were not only seen but fully *known*.

PRAYER PROMPT

Lord, help me to reflect on the depth of your knowledge of me. You know my deepest pains, my darkest sins, my greatest

*hopes—and you love and accept me fully. In the moments where
I long to be seen, remind me that your knowing is greater. Amen.*

Name 3. Needy: Deeply Embedded Names
Scripture Reading: Genesis 5:1-2

Each of us can recall being called a name that we did not want to
embrace as ours. *Stupid. Lazy. Selfish. Needy.* We all have names
that call out to our soul in the very moments we think we've moved
beyond them. And while we are meant to do away with some of
these negative names completely, other names are invitations—
meant to be captured and reframed.

Without the name *Needy*, for instance, we can start to believe a
dangerous narrative: that somehow, we are the ones in charge of the
details of our lives and then, in the places where life isn't what we
want, that *we must try and hustle harder.* Some of us need to claim
the name Needy (or something like it) for ourselves because we have
refused to rely on God's sovereignty. Others might need to remove
the shame that coats this name. We need to realize that being needy
is not a negative; it's part of being human. It is the one name that
will move us toward relying on the Lord in a deeper, more true way.

QUESTIONS

1. Have you or someone else ever described yourself with
   a negative name like Needy? What kind of emotional
   connotations does that bring up?

2. In what ways do you need to reconstruct your idea of that
   name? Where does God want to redeem or reframe a name
   that you've struggled with?

3. How can you invite God to tend to the false names you've gone by?

4. What does our culture believe about the name Needy, or other names like it? Why are these seen as negative traits?

5. What is the connection between humility and acknowledging our need? Why is it so hard to admit to ourselves, others, and God that we are limited human beings?

6. How would living with the understanding that we cannot operate independently of others or God change how we move in the world? How can this bring freedom in our lives?

There may be broken names that you have clung to over the years that God is asking you to hand over to him. Names that may have shaped your mind and spirit into believing lies that aren't true. Some of those names need to be done away with completely, but some need to be reconstructed by the Spirit—renovated into a name that truly fits.

PRAYER PROMPT

Lord, release the broken names that I have been clinging on to for far too long. Heal the names that ring out lies and speak false narratives about who I am. And, in your mercy, please reframe the names that I've deemed negative, the ones that you want to deem redemptive. Amen.

Name 4. Unveiled: Ooze and Bones
Scripture Reading: Ezekiel 37:4-6; 2 Corinthians 3:3, 18; 4:10

In a world hiding behind perfectly curated images of who we want others to think we are, the idea of being unveiled may feel a bit scary. Our messy and unfinished places being exposed can seem too vulnerable. And yet when we are witnessed, known, fully unveiled . . . we best begin to see and reflect God's glory.

When we allow God to remove all the pretense and propaganda we use to cover ourselves and all the muddled, chaotic emotions and the issues we carry, he gives us something that covering up never does: *freedom.* It's freedom to let our whole selves be seen and known; to allow God to meet us here in the sea of doubts we wrestle with; and to lay down all our fears, our struggles, and our imperfections at the altar of his grace.

In our unveiling, we undergo a transformation: We become *who we already are.* A metamorphosis into a luminous, Christlike creature. Like the butterfly who quietly transforms in the hidden darkness, we, too, must experience the struggle and resistance that somehow produces a glorious, beautiful revolution.

QUESTIONS

1. What are some of the "issues" you try to hide from God and others? How do you usually approach your issues? What is your inner dialogue when these things are brought to your attention?

2. In what ways have you seen a transformation in yourself through the pains and struggles you have faced? How has suffering brought a metamorphosis into Christ's likeness?

3. How do you handle the tension of where you are now and who you are becoming? How does knowing you are *unveiled* help as you recognize the paradox of spiritual formation, in which you are in the process of becoming who Christ has already said you are?

4. How can suffering be transformative? Why is wrestling such an important part of the process in the life of a believer?

5. How do you think the church as a whole is at holding space for the metamorphosis that is taking place in each of our lives? How can we better allow for people to be both a finished work and a work in progress?

6. How has someone else's story of pain and growing into Christ's likeness encouraged you in your own? How can your story be an encouragement to someone else?

As you reflect on your own "corner of issues," the ones that you try to hide and keep from view, remember that the veil has been lifted. You can live both as a completed work and simultaneously as one in process, without shame or resistance. All because of this: Through the work of Christ on your behalf, you are *unveiled*.

PRAYER PROMPT

Lord, in the dark, hidden cocoon in which you are transforming me through pain and suffering, teach me the beauty that is here. Help me to see the process that you've designed, transforming me into the likeness of Jesus as a grace and a gift, even when it is painful and hard. Let me live unveiled, not hiding behind the curtain of my own fears and doubts but reveling in your presence through whatever issues I am facing. Amen.

Name 5. *Whole: Defined by Victory*

Scripture Reading: Genesis 1:27; Matthew 13:53-58; Luke 8:40-48

Fear of being defined by your pain, your trauma, or your sickness can keep you from revealing the hard pieces of your story. None of us want to be seen as the victim, so we can try to hide the difficulties we've endured. But suppressing pain can keep us from the very healing Jesus offers.

The suffering woman believed that a mere brush of Jesus' hem could bring her relief. And she was right. When the crowds were pushing in on him from every which way, he immediately felt this woman graze against his cloak. He could tell that *power* had gone out from him. His disciples thought he was crazy to try to figure out who had touched him, but Jesus' only concern was the woman who needed him.

In that moment, this unseen, ostracized woman, who had suffered with this ailment of bleeding for years, had the most important eyes in the world on her. She was healed because of her faith in what Christ could do. She believed that this Messiah really cared about someone like her. To him, this woman was not defined by the suffering she had carried for so long. No—the only name, the only definition that mattered, was that she was *God's daughter*. In this one interaction with Jesus, she became *whole*.

QUESTIONS

1. What are some of your "just a _____" statements?

2. Where do you need to exchange feelings of rejection for the truth that you are a child of God? How does being God's son or daughter change the definitions you've carried?

3. How do you define "wholeness"?

4. Read Mark 5:24-34. What stands out to you most in this story? In what ways can you identify with the woman who bled for years and just wanted to touch Jesus?

5. What are some hurts that you long for that kind of healing from?

6. Why is it important to share the ways in which Jesus *has* healed us in our story? How can that help bring others to healing and faith in Christ?

7. How is Jesus' example in the face of rejection from those in his hometown helpful to us in our own? How could you use that as a way to move through your own story, in which you live out of approval from God rather than humans?

A hurt child finds security, comfort, and restoration in the arms of a loving mother or father. They are protected. Held. Healed. Made Whole. That is what our Abba gives us as we rest close to his chest in the middle of our deepest pains. As you wrestle through your heartaches, don't forget the most important thing about you: *You have victory in Jesus.*

PRAYER PROMPT

Lord, as I seek your healing in my life, remind me that you are my healer. Show me, in my moments of desperation, when I try to find healing in other places, that you are a safe place to come and stretch out my arms to. One touch of your garment brings wholeness and restoration. Teach me to ground myself in the security of knowing that I am yours. Amen.

Name 6. (Re)Named: God Names Us Forward

Scripture Reading: Genesis 17:1-7, 15-16; 32:24-30; Psalm 8:4-5; Hosea 1:10–2:1; 1 Peter 2:10

What do you call a man who faithfully pledged his allegiance to a friend until the very end, no matter what's to come, only to falter before the morning's light? *Rock*. It's not the name I would choose for a guy who betrayed Jesus so easily, refusing to even entertain the idea of his own soul's folly. And yet *Rock* was the name Jesus gave Peter, a forward name, a foretelling of *who he would become*. Peter means *rock*. A foundation upon which Christ would build his church.

Peter is in good company with the forward names bestowed on some of the giants of our faith: Abraham, Sarah, Hosea and Gomer's children, and Jacob. The Lord has long been in the business of changing names to not only display the becoming but also to reveal the work he is doing in the lives of those whose names he replaced.

Like the spiritual heroes of the Bible, we, too, have a new name, one God has given us in anticipation of who we will be.

We may learn this name from a label that we would rather not have but that teaches and refines us. It may come in the form of rejecting the past names we've answered to. And it may come after sitting in silence, asking the Lord to show us the birth certificate he has filled out on our behalf. Whatever way your new name comes, remember that God's name matters most.

QUESTIONS

1. Pray and brainstorm a bit. What might be a name that God has given you? What name might God want to speak over you in order to call forward who you are becoming?

2. What are some false or hurtful names that God has revealed to you that he wants to do away with? How might some of the names you've carried be a part of who God is making you into?

3. In what ways is God redeeming parts of your story? What names have you allowed your life to be defined by for too long? What names can become a part of a redemptive narrative in your life?

4. How can the idea of being *named forward* be an encouragement in the life of a believer?

5. In what ways are we called to become *like Christ*? What are some verses that reveal who we are to become?

6. Why is a change in identity such a gift for most of us? How can someone else seeing who we will become help us move toward that end?

You may have lived your life trying to shake a name, a nickname, or a label that seemed to cling to you no matter how hard you tried to lose it. The good news is that each of us, no matter what names our past might hold, are given the gift of a new one, a name of who we are becoming in Christ. Each of us gets the gift of being called forward into redemption with a fresh designation, unlike any we've ever had.

PRAYER PROMPT

Lord, more important than who I was is who you are making me into. As past names and labels haunt my spirit, let me be reminded of the forward name that you have bestowed on me. In your eyes, I look like Christ, even here in the middle of my wrestling with sin and my flesh. Let that knowledge of the power of your renaming be an encouragement to me as I seek to live up to my new name. Amen.

Part II: Whose You Are

Name 7. God's Child: Recognizing God's Voice
Scripture Reading: Genesis 9:6; Ezekiel 4:4-8; Luke 20:36; John 8:1-11; 20:11-18

Some words, no matter how tough our skin, are sharp enough to pierce us. Words that belittle, degrade, and demean. Words that shrink us. They are the ones we play over and over in our minds, concocting imaginary scenarios in which we fought back and proved wrong the verdict we'd been handed.

When the words of another cut deep into the muscle of our hearts, we need immediate assistance to stop the bleeding. The only balm and bandage that can stave off the hemorrhaging flow is being reminded of the status bestowed on us: *Child of God.*

Repeating that name to ourselves reminds us that it is the opinion of the One who created both the offended and the offender that matters.

QUESTIONS

1. When has someone's words deeply wounded you? How has another's assessment of your gifts, your talents, or *who you are* caused you to shrink?

2. In what ways have you seen Jesus change your name from *condemned* to *free*? In what ways do you want to reject the judgments of others in exchange for the acceptance of Christ?

3. How does seeing God as a loving parent change your perspective on how to handle criticism and critique from

others? How can this help you discern what correction is from the Lord and what is not?

4. Read John 8:1-11. What does Jesus do in response to the angry mob? What do you think this tells us about how we are supposed to respond to the sins or inadequacies of others? What affect do you think Jesus' response had on the woman in the story?

5. Why is relational credit so important when it comes to speaking into the lives of others? Why does protecting another's humanity before we offer correction matter?

6. How do you think the church can better model the example of Christ in John 8? What bearing might that have in terms of seeing repentance come in our culture?

We are but dust. And the minute we forget that, we lose the power to help shape and mold, and instead we scatter one another into tiny bits. We must remember that our God isn't one to come hammering down on us, breaking us. No—we have a God who gets down on the ground and starts stirring the dust at the feet of those who are ready to convict us. He is the one who bends low and protects our humanity from those who want to rip it apart. That kind of love changes us. That kind of love drowns out the name-calling from schoolyard bullies with the affectionate call of a father and mother for their child.

PRAYER PROMPT

Lord, sometimes I equate the sound of those who are bent on criticizing, demeaning, or silencing me with your voice. Remind me that you speak to me not like the angry mob

hell-bent on my destruction but rather as a loving parent,
determined to protect and love. Let me become so aware of
your tone that I can quickly recover from the declarations of
those who try to convince me they are speaking on your behalf.
Amen.

Name 8. *God's Living Statues: Our Iconoclast God*
Scripture Reading: Genesis 1:26; Exodus 20:4-6; Deuteronomy
5:8-10; 1 Peter 2:5

What does it mean to be an image bearer of God? Each of us, with
all our uniqueness and differences, is a small representation of a
piece of God. This is why, when people—women, children, eth-
nic minorities, and many others—are abused and degraded, God's
heart is grieved. For within each one of those mistreated souls lies
the precious image of God.

Though the *imago Dei* within us cannot be diminished, often-
times, we allow others to make us feel like it is. The false narratives
we've been given about who we are and our place in this world
causes us to hide the parts of us that God made uniquely, parts that
show a piece of God every time they see the light.

And yet there is nothing truer about us than *how we were made*.
In God's very own image. A representation of *who* God is right
here in tangible presence. Shine forth bravely *who you are*, sharing
your voice, your gifts, and yourself. You are offering the world a
picture of God.

QUESTIONS

1. What are some ways God uniquely made you? How does
   that reveal a piece of who God is?

2. What fears do you have when it comes to revealing your true self to others?

3. What reflections of God does the world need right now? How can you embody the essence of the Lord in your sphere of influence?

4. How has sin or shame distorted the way we bear God's image?

5. Where have you seen people represent and reflect God's presence, his power, his compassion, and his authority on earth? What was the impact on their environment and community?

6. Why does understanding *imago Dei* matter so much in this cultural moment? How can the church help to honor the God-given essence in all of humanity? In what ways has the church failed in this? Where do you see hope and change?

7. How can you encourage someone else to embrace their *imago Dei*? How can acknowledging it in one another be a path toward healing? How can we call forth creativity and growth in the life of someone else?

It can be hard to live in such a way that you allow the *imago Dei* within you and within others to be seen, honored, and celebrated. As we push through our past hurts and the words that wounded us, or the experiences that caused us to hide pieces of ourselves, we can be tempted to cover up the very essence of who we are. But doing so not only hurts our own souls; it keeps others from seeing, up close and personal, a part of God. In a world easily distracted by counterfeits, show the people around you a living statue of the one true God.

Lord, let me be your living statue. Let the imago Dei *within me shine forth, giving others a glimpse of who you are in how you've made me. Let them see it in my voice, my creativity, my leadership, my gifts, and my faith in Jesus. Let them see it in how I handle my pain and my struggles. Let them see it in all the ways I hold space in this world. In your name, amen.*

Name 9. God's Likeness: The Spitting Image
Scripture Reading: Genesis 5:1-5; Romans 12:5

Seeing ourselves like God sees us, as the spitting image of Jesus, can be hard. To live out of our likeness, we must internalize the gospel of Christ more and more with each step. Seeing others in that same light can be a challenge as we argue and disagree about a wide range of topics and ideas. And yet we are called to both: seeing ourselves and seeing others in God's likeness.

We've been created in God's image substantively, functionally, and relationally. Something about our substance, how we function in the world, and how we are to move through our relationships, is meant to reflect God—individually and collectively. And that truth has the power to break through the incorrect dogma that tells us to hold onto shame in our brokenness.

Many of us have had to confront a theology of unworthiness, one that overemphasizes our sin, our brokenness, our failures. It's this theology that the gospel longs to confront. Though your sin separated you from God, it no longer defines you: The blood shed on your behalf not only reconciles you to God but he now sees you just as he sees his perfect Son.

QUESTIONS

1. What are some of the functional ways we have been created in God's image? In what ways have you seen this twisted by a culture or society?

2. How has the church not fully expressed the reflection of God's love relationally? In what ways have we overstated the importance of some relationships (like marriage and parenthood) and understated the importance of others (like spiritual parent or friend)? How can that cause pain to those who haven't experienced the types of relationships most discussed in the context of church?

3. How can the church better display and celebrate the likeness of God to the world?

4. How do you see yourself in relationship to God? Have you learned to overemphasize your sin and brokenness, or do you view yourself through the lens of Christ's likeness?

5. When have you felt as if you had to clean yourself up or *be better* before you could come before God? What teachings or voices in your life have steered you wrongly in this direction?

6. How should we talk about sin while also holding onto what God has said about the dignity of all humans?

7. How does seeing God's likeness in humanity as a whole help you to get a bigger picture of God's image?

Being made in the likeness of God is about more than merely a transfer of divine qualities onto ourselves. It means that in Christ, we are given access to the deepest level of relational intimacy with the one who created us. His love and his presence are imputed over our lives in spite of the sin that separated us from it. And through that, we can see ourselves from the same lens as he uses: holy, loved, and made new.

Lord, forgive us for the ways we have demeaned, abused, dishonored, and devalued those made in your image. Forgive us for the ways we've done that to ourselves. Teach us to treat one another as those who carry within them your likeness. Help us bring that forth in ourselves. In your name we pray, amen.

Name 10. *God's Found One: Seen in the Wasteland*

Scripture Reading: Genesis 16; 21; Exodus 3; 4:1-5; Ephesians 4:24

Have you ever been lost? I mean *really* lost? Unsure of which way you should turn, trying to figure out which direction you are supposed to head . . . and then, all of a sudden, a kind stranger notices your bewilderment and offers to show you the way? When a guide arrives, so does a sense of relief and peace.

In our wilderness, we experience the panic of pacing in every which way, hoping to be found so that we can feel God's presence in the midst of it. Like Hagar and Moses, we want to be pursued and invited to meet I Am.

But sometimes instead of accepting that invitation, we live in a stubborn belief that God isn't able to search us out in the vastness of the desert in which we find ourselves. We forget that there is no place on this earth he cannot find, no situation he is not able to lead us through. Whatever you are facing, whether unprecedented times or feeling lost, remember that God is in the business of seeking, not hiding. Remember that you are known and seen by God. You will always be found when you feel lost and afraid.

QUESTIONS

1. How have you tried to make God too confined, too small, too domesticated, or too tame? What could remind you of how big God truly is?

2. In your wasteland, how have you experienced *El Roi*, the God who sees?

3. How can knowing that you are pursued by the God of the universe give you comfort in the desert?

4. Read Genesis 16. In what ways is Hagar pursued and found? Why is the name she gives God so powerful?

5. Recall a story you have heard about God showing up in another person's wilderness. Why are those stories so important to the body of Christ?

6. Think about some collective deserts we have endured. How has the Lord pursued and sought out the church in and through them?

When you look out at the immensity of your wilderness, it can be easy to believe that God cannot find you there. That perhaps you are too far gone, too hidden in the distance between you and him. Let yourself remember that our God isn't limited by time and space like we are. When you feel alone and wandering, he is there, meeting you with his presence to let you know that *you are found.*

Lord, you are the God who pursues, who seeks, who finds. In my wandering in uncertain and uncharted terrain, you are my search party. Let me not confine you to a small box, but let me rejoice in your vastness that supersedes any desert I may find myself in. Amen.

Part III: How It Changes Everything

Name 11. *You Are the Currency of the Kingdom: Made for God's Purposes*
Scripture Reading: Psalm 23; Mark 12:13-17

Our culture loves a good restoration. We watch reality shows about old, rusty cars made shiny and new or a home-improvement series in which the worst house on the block is magically transformed into the best one. And while we love to watch these changes unfold in the course of thirty minutes or less, we often underestimate the sacrifice that goes into turning these old, abandoned relics into shiny, better than before, restorations.

No matter the season of life we are in and regardless of what we are going through, the Spirit of God tenderly utilizes each new life phase to reconstruct us, to make us more and more like him. It is through ongoing seasons of surrender that the most beautiful image gets forged in our lives: *Christ in us*.

QUESTIONS

1. What are some seasons that left you feeling hidden or like you were going backward? How do you tend to stay stuck in

the past, or are you a futurist? Is God asking you to embrace a new season? If so, how do you know?

2. As you look at your current life phase, what is God inviting you into that is different than past ones? How can you fully embrace this invitation?

3. Read Psalm 23. How does God the Shepherd bring restoration according to these verses? When have you seen that in your own life or in the life of a loved one?

4. Take a look at the appendix about the names of God. How does knowing the names of God encourage you? What names of God are meaningful to you in your current stage and season of life and why?

5. Who is someone who comes to mind that exemplifies this idea of being restored through the sacrifice and surrender over their lifetime? How does that encourage you?

As you think about the ways God is forging you in the "hidden seasons" or in each new season, remember that like a good shepherd, God is always leading you forward into new pastures. When new junctures come your way, ask God to help you see the ways the Spirit is inviting you to be restored in them.

PRAYER PROMPT

Lord, it is so easy to get stuck. Past seasons of hardship or new seasons of facing the unknown can sometimes make me feel afraid and anxious. Help me accept the invitation into the restoration you desire to do within me, revealing your image and inscription on my life. In your name I pray, amen.

Name 12. *You Are a Name Giver: Ruling, Blessing, and Naming*
Scripture Reading: Genesis 1:28; 14:18-20; Psalm 110:4; Hebrews 7;
1 Peter 2:9-10

Every expectant parent knows the pressure that can come with choosing a name. *Should it be a family one? Does it need to be deep and meaningful? Does it sound good? Will it fit who they are?* Being the one tasked with naming can feel big. But while the act itself is not what matters, the *way* in which we name does.

Seeing in others their true name, being the one to call it out and bring it to their attention, is a sacred gift we can give one another. We have the opportunity to bless others by calling out the ways we see the Lord manifesting himself in them.

Through the example of our High Priest, Jesus, the one who bestows a name on us, we, too, can speak honor and dignity over the lives we encounter. We can attune ourselves to point out the very names God has given another: *teacher, leader, friend, warrior.* And by doing so, we set a feast of encouragement before them.

QUESTIONS

1. When have you experienced someone *naming you* in a way that built your spirit up?

2. Have you ever named another in response to what you see in them? How was that offering received?

3. How can you ask Jesus to help you become more aware of the ways he wants you to name those around you? Who is he asking you to speak a name of honor and dignity over?

4. Take some time to be very real with God. What false, negative, or dehumanizing names have you spoken over others (loved ones, neighbors, strangers)? Take some time to confess and repent of that today.

5. How does the example of the royal priest setting out a table of bread and wine of hospitality, praising God, and naming others frame your perspective as you consider your own role as a royal priest?

6. Where do you see the calling of a royal priest most needed in the world right now?

Learning to be a person who speaks dignifying goodness about and over others is something this generation longs for. Most people can tell you the names they were given by those around them—names that cut, names that wounded, names they still carry years after the first utterance of them. Our world is longing for an encouraging word that calls out someone's innate value and worth. Which is why we must not forget that like Jesus, our High Priest, we have the opportunity to name as an act of blessing and a way to draw people to the Great High Namer.

PRAYER PROMPT

Lord, help me attune to your spirit so that as I go about my days, I can see the goodness in others. May I be like you, naming what I see aloud. Let my words encourage and strengthen those who are discouraged, downhearted, and dismayed. Help me see and celebrate the ways you have uniquely gifted another so that they can stand firm in who they are in you. Amen.

Name 13. *You Are Sent: Living Your Name*
Scripture Reading: Psalm 101; Jeremiah 29:5-7; Zechariah 4:10

Our name gives us a sense of who we are and a sense of belonging. It identifies us. It calls forth something inside of us. And through it, we become known. As you reflect on the names you've been given throughout your life, the ones that threatened to undermine your identity and the ones that fortified you in a deeper understanding of *whose* you were, ask God to show you your calling from them.

It's from the outflow of our names that we live out a life of service. From a place of love and acceptance, we can begin to see our inner transformation result in an outward, authentic, humble servant, bent on using our unique giftedness to bring glory to God alone. The culmination of life experience, natural abilities, wholehearted passions, life stage, personality, and location can start to uncover a new name: that of Kingdom worker, sent and empowered to serve.

The old adage that *Everything happens for a reason* may have some validity when it comes to looking at your life. Everything you have gone through—all the failures, winding trails, and opportunities—helps you live into your new names: *Called* and *Sent*.

QUESTIONS

1. As you look at your life—your passions, your location, your opportunities, life stage, and personality, what are some ways God has uniquely positioned you to serve and love people? What may be the distinct Kingdom work God has given you?

2. What are some ways you can stay faithful to your calling, especially in the hidden and unseen times in which God is developing your character?

3. What ministry do you see your life moving you toward? (It may be in a formal way or it could be by serving in those places where you already have access and influence.)

4. What are some ways that you have seen people live out their calling that aren't in the traditional form of church-based ministries?

5. What is the connection between integrity and calling? Why does character matter so much when it comes to our ministry work?

6. What is your Christian community being called to do? How can you move toward that calling with others?

So many of our names are passively ascribed to us. They require nothing from us but to accept them as our own. While those names form the foundation of our inner posture, they should result in a desire to move, to do, to serve. To be called and sent is not a mantle we simply pick up without any assistance or guidance but rather one that—through humble prayer and honest evaluation of ourselves and our lives—we can begin to see God illuminate the path of Kingdom work that he has laid just for us. May we boldly step out as sent and called, bringing God glory each step of the way.

PRAYER PROMPT

Lord, help me pay attention to the ways you have uniquely shaped and formed my life and named me—who I am. Reveal how you desire to use all of me: my failures and weaknesses as well as my strengths and experiences to fulfill your call of a greater Kingdom purpose on my life. Let me be sensitive to the opportunities you've set before me and keep my heart from fear, insecurity, and a lack of integrity so that I can become the great fisher of men and women that you've asked me to be. In your name, amen.

Name 14. *He Is the Name Above Every Other: The Name of Jesus*
Scripture Reading: Psalm 110:1; Isaiah 53; Mark 10:45; John 20:30-31; Romans 5:12-21; 2 Corinthians 5:21; Philippians 2:1-11; Colossians 1:15; Hebrews 2:14-15; 1 Peter 1:16; 1 John 3:8; 1 John 4:7-10; Revelation 21:5

Even though our names are powerful, only one name has the power to change every piece of our world: the name of Jesus. Through that name, you are rescued, redeemed, and restored. The name of Jesus forms the foundation and the transformation of all other names.

No other name can even compare. You are known because he longs to know you. As you seek to understand your own names, remember that the uniqueness and beauty of your identity has profound significance *only* because of the name of the one who made you.

QUESTIONS

1. Of all the names you read about in this book, which is most meaningful to you? Why?

2. What are some ways God is calling you to use the names he has given you?

3. Think of the names you have read about. What would they mean without the name of Jesus?

4. How does *not* trying to make a name for ourselves but using our names to bless others go against the current culture?

5. What names do you think the world struggles to understand the most? Why are so many people's identity skewed?

6. What is your greatest takeaway when it comes to this idea of names and naming? How will you live your life differently because of it?

7. You are known by God, intimately. Stop to consider that incredible truth. What does that mean to you? How does that "change everything"?

8. The name of Jesus changes everything. How has Jesus changed your understanding of your own "namedness"?

Through the Spirit's work in our lives, we are able to become more and more like Christ, shedding the false names and identities we have collected throughout the years and instead living into a true, lasting one. But this identity isn't to just serve our fragile ego—it is to embolden us so that we may bless every person we encounter. Your life and your names exist to point yourself and the world around you toward the greatest truth: that in all our brokenness, our hurt, and our sin, there is but one name above it all. *Jesus.*

PRAYER PROMPT

Lord, help me internalize all the names you've given me so that through them, I can grow in the image of Christ. When I am hurting, help me look to Jesus. Show me the names I need to remind myself of most, names like Beloved, Known, Seen, Child of God, Imago. Let me rest securely, with my identity firmly rooted, in the one name that matters, the name above all names: Jesus. Amen.

NOTES

FOREWORD: UNNAMED

1. "Global Findings," Global Slavery Index, accessed March 11, 2021, https://www.globalslaveryindex.org/2018/findings/global-findings /#:~:text=An%20estimated%2040.3%20million%20men,up%2071%20 percent%20of%20victims.
2. "UNICEF: Too Many Children Dying of Malnutrition," UNICEF USA, accessed March 11, 2021, https://www.unicefusa.org/press/releases/unicef -too-many-children-dying-malnutrition/8259.
3. "Figures at a Glance," UNHCR, June 18, 2020, https://www.unhcr.org /figures-at-a-glance.html.
4. Hannah Ritchie and Max Roser, "Natural Disasters," revised November 2019, https://www.ourworldindata.org/natural-disasters.
5. "Mental Health and Substance Abuse," World Health Organization, accessed March 11, 2021, https://www.who.int/teams/mental-health-and -substance-use/suicide-data.
6. "Statistics," International Center for Assault Prevention, accessed March 11, 2021, https://www.internationalcap.org/abuse-neglect-info/statistics/.
7. "WHO Coronavirus (COVID-19) Dashboard," accessed March 11, 2021, https://covid19.who.int/.
8. "Breast Cancer Statistics," Komen, accessed March 11, 2021, https://www .komen.org/breast-cancer/facts-statistics/breast-cancer-statistics/.

AS WE BEGIN: A QUESTION

1. David Gates, "Aubrey," *Guitar Man* © 1972 Elektra.
2. "Aubrey Origin and Meaning," accessed February 15, 2021, https://www .nameberry.com/babyname/Aubrey/girl. Slightly paraphrased.
3. "Aubrey," accessed February 15, 2021, https://www.names-of-baby.com /browser/g/aubrey.html#.YAsiCi1h3_Q.
4. Online Etymology Dictionary, s.v. "name, *n.*," accessed February 15, 2021, https://www.etymonline.com/word/name.
5. Emily P. Freeman, "Leave It Behind," August 4, 2020, in *The Next Right Thing Podcast*, 6:55, https://www.emilypfreeman.com/podcast/138/.

6. Ruth Haley Barton, *Strengthening the Soul of Your Leadership: Seeking God in the Crucible of Ministry* (Downers Grove, IL: IVP Books, 2018), 79.

NAME 1: BELOVED: DID GOD REALLY SAY?

1. James K. A. Smith, *On the Road with Saint Augustine: A Real-World Spirituality for Restless Hearts* (Grand Rapids, MI: Brazos Press, 2019), 13.
2. Scot McKnight and Laura Barringer, *A Church Called Tov: Forming a Goodness Culture That Resists Abuses of Power and Promotes Healing* (Carol Stream, IL: Tyndale Momentum, 2020), 8–9.
3. STEP Bible, "beloved," accessed March 15, 2021, https://www.stepbible .org/?q=version=ESV|strong=G0027&options=VHNUG.
4. Blue Letter Bible, "Lexicon: Strong's H2896—ṭôḇ," accessed March 16, 2021, https://www.blueletterbible.org/lang/lexicon/lexicon. cfm?Strongs=H2896&t=NIV.
5. Henri J. M. Nouwen, *Life of the Beloved: Spiritual Living in a Secular World* (New York: Crossroad, 1992), 33.
6. STEP Bible, "crafty," Genesis 3:1, accessed February 16, 2021, https:// www.stepbible.org/?q=reference=Gen.3&options=VHNUG.
7. Lecrae (@lecrae), "The devil has a plot but God has a plan," Instagram, January 21, 2021.
8. Gustaf Aulén, *Christus Victor: An Historical Study of the Idea of the Three Main Types of the Idea of Atonement*, trans. A. G. Hebert (Eugene, OR: Wipf & Stock, 2003), 4.
9. Rick Richardson, *Experiencing Healing Prayer: How God Turns Our Hearts into Wholeness* (Downers Grove, IL: InterVarsity Press, 2005), 103.

NAME 2: KNOWN: GOD NAMES US BACKWARD

1. I learned about this practice from a professor in my graduate school program, Jayna Gallagher. I do not know if it's original to her.
2. These were the instructions given to the class from Jayna Gallagher, a guest professor in our graduate school program. Jayna Gallagher, "Personal Leadership and Development" (video lecture for Wheaton College Graduate School on schoology.com, January 2021).
3. William Shakespeare, *Romeo and Juliet*, Act III, Scene II, lines 21–25.

NAME 3: NEEDY: DEEPLY EMBEDDED NAMES

1. As cited by Ashlee Eiland in her book *Human(Kind): How Reclaiming Human Worth and Embracing Radical Kindness Will Bring Us Back Together* (Colorado Springs: Waterbrook, 2020), 51.
2. John F. Kilner, *Dignity and Destiny: Humanity in the Image of God* (Grand Rapids, MI: Eerdmans, 2015), 102. In it, he writes, "By yielding to the temptation, Adam and Eve do indeed become like God by knowing good

and evil (Gen. 3.22). In context, this appears to be a reference to gaining autonomy—taking upon themselves the responsibility for distinguishing good and evil."

3. Kilner writes, "Dependence on God is central to what creation in God's image entails," *Dignity and Destiny*, 102.

NAME 4: UNVEILED: OOZE AND BONES

1. Ferris Jabr, "How Does a Caterpillar Turn into a Butterfly?," *Scientific American*, August 10, 2012, https://www.scientificamerican.com/article /caterpillar-butterfly-metamorphosis-explainer/#:~:text=One%20day%2 C%20the%20caterpillar%20stops,as%20a%20butterfly%20or%20moth.

2. Jabr, "How Does a Caterpillar Turn into a Butterfly?"

3. Jen Wilkin says, "Sanctification is the process of joyfully growing luminous," in her book *In His Image: 10 Ways God Calls Us to Reflect His Character* (Wheaton, IL: Crossway, 2018), 153.

NAME 5: WHOLE: DEFINED BY VICTORY

1. See my first book, *Overcomer: Breaking Down the Walls of Shame and Rebuilding Your Soul* (Grand Rapids, MI: Zondervan, 2015).

2. Elizabeth Gilbert, *Big Magic: Creative Living Beyond Fear* (New York: Riverhead Books, 2016), 14. In it, Gilbert writes, "You're afraid you're too fat. (I don't know what this has to do with creativity, exactly, but experience has taught me that most of us are afraid we're too fat, so let's just put that on the anxiety list, for good measure.)"

NAME 6: (RE)NAMED: GOD NAMES US FORWARD

1. Shared with permission.

2. *Dignity and Destiny: Humanity in the Image of God* (Grand Rapids, MI: Eerdmans, 2015) is an incredible scholarly work by John F. Kilner. You'll see that I've cited Kilner several times in this book. Kilner's title stuck with me so much that you'll also find the phrase "dignity and destiny" scattered throughout.

3. Emmanuel M. Katongole, "'Threatened with Resurrection': Martyrdom and Reconciliation in the World Church," in *Witness of the Body: The Past, Present, and Future of Christian Martyrdom*, ed. Michael L. Budde and Karen Scott (Grand Rapids, MI: Eerdmans, 2011), 197.

4. Mark Batterson says something similar about the stories we tell ourselves in his book *Win the Day: 7 Daily Habits to Help You Stress Less and Accomplish More* (Colorado Springs: Multnomah, 2020), 8: "The difference between success and failure is the stories we tell ourselves. . . . Why does God give us a new name? It's His way of flipping the script."

5. In this section, I'm taking some creative liberties with the biblical accounts,

imagining how Abram-turned-Abraham may have felt about God's extraordinary plan for him and his wife and similarly how Hosea and Jacob would have responded to their name-change moments.

NAME 7: GOD'S CHILD: RECOGNIZING GOD'S VOICE
1. STEP Bible, s.v. "(*a.dam*) 'man' (H0120)," accessed February 19, 2021, https://www.stepbible.org/?q=strong=H0120|version=ESV&options=HV NUG&qFilter=H0120.
2. Karl Barth, *The Humanity of God* (Louisville: Westminster John Knox Press, 1996), 53.

NAME 8: GOD'S LIVING STATUES: OUR ICONOCLAST GOD
1. Martin Buber, *Tales of the Hasidim* (New York: Schocken Books, 1991), 251.
2. "Image and Likeness," in *NIV Cultural Backgrounds Study Bible* (Grand Rapids, MI: Zondervan, 2016), 8.
3. Jen Wilkin says, "On the sixth day of creation, the rhythm of the narrative noticeably breaks. 'Let there be' becomes 'Let us make'"; *In His Image: 10 Ways God Calls Us to Reflect His Character* (Wheaton, IL: Crossway, 2018), 15.

NAME 9: GOD'S LIKENESS: THE SPITTING IMAGE
1. "Spitting Image," Phrase Finder, accessed March 2, 2021, https://www.phrases.org.uk/meanings/spitting-image.html.
2. John Mark Comer, *Garden City: Work, Rest, and the Art of Being Human* (Grand Rapids, MI: Zondervan, 2015), 61. Here, Comer writes, "We're called to a very specific kind of work. To make a Garden-like world where image bearers can flourish and thrive, where people can experience and enjoy God's generous love."
3. Swiss theologian Karl Barth made this concept famous. See Karl Barth, *Church Dogmatics Volume III: The Doctrine of Creation*, ed. Geoffrey W. Bromiley and Thomas F. Torrance (Edinburgh: T&T Clark, 1958), 220.
4. St. Gregory of Nyssa, "On the Making of Man," accessed March 3, 2021, https://www.newadvent.org/fathers/2914.htm.
5. Jemar Tisby, *How to Fight Racism: Courageous Christianity and the Journey Toward Racial Justice* (Grand Rapids, MI: Zondervan, 2021), 28–29.
6. Paul Brand and Philip Yancey, *Fearfully and Wonderfully Made: The Marvel of Bearing God's Image* (Downers Grove, IL: InterVarsity Press, 2019), 44.
7. Lin-Manuel Miranda, "The Schuyler Sisters," *Hamilton: An American Musical* © 2015 Atlantic. (The musical came out on Disney+ as I was writing this book, and the incredible soundtrack was constantly stuck in my head. If you're not a fan, sorry not sorry.)
8. John F. Kilner, *Dignity and Destiny: Humanity in the Image of God* (Grand

Rapids, MI: Eerdmans, 2015), 175. Here, Kilner offers a list of many terms that are often used to describe the "damaged" image of God, including terms like *lost, obliterated, destroyed*, etc.

9. Julian of Norwich, *Revelations of Divine Love*, trans. Elizabeth Spearing (Suffolk: Penguin Random House, 1998), 49.

NAME 10: GOD'S FOUND ONE: SEEN IN THE WASTELAND

1. Kimmy Yam, "Anti-Asian Hate Crimes Increased by Nearly 150% in 2020, Mostly in N.Y. and L.A., New Report Says," NBC News, March 9, 2021, https://www.nbcnews.com/news/asian-america/anti-asian-hate-crimes -increased-nearly-150-2020-mostly-n-n1260264.

2. "Rare Wolverine Spotted in Pacific County," May 28, 2020, video on YouTube, https://www.youtube.com/watch?v=nwLWm81I0co.

3. Lisa Bevere (@lisabevere), "God's pursuit *is greater than* your ability to wander," Instagram, March 10, 2021, https://www.instagram.com/p /CMPq8Jus_lD/?utm_source=ig_web_copy_link.

4. Beth Felker Jones, *Practicing Christian Doctrine: An Introduction to Thinking and Living Theologically* (Grand Rapids, MI: Baker Academic, 2014), 132.

NAME 11: YOU ARE THE CURRENCY OF THE KINGDOM: MADE FOR GOD'S PURPOSES

1. To see a picture of this painting, visit http://www.arthursussmangallery.com /jacobangel.htm.

2. In the conclusion to Jen Wilkin's book *In His Image: 10 Ways God Calls Us to Reflect His Character* (Wheaton, IL: Crossway, 2018), 147–53, called "Engraved with His Image," she also cites the story of Jesus' conversation and writes about coins and the image of God.

3. Wilkin, *In His Image*, 153.

4. Elizabeth Gilbert, *Big Magic: Creative Living Beyond Fear* (New York: Riverhead Books, 2016), 5.

5. Christine Caine (@christinecaine), in her Instagram post on January 23, 2021, shared an image quote that says, "Don't confuse invisibility with insignificance," https://www.instagram.com/p/CKaCbdOjBAX /?utm_source=ig_web_copy_link.

6. Beth Moore (@BethMooreLPM), "True greatness will never come . . . ," Twitter, July 18, 2020, https://www.twitter.com/BethMooreLPM/status /1284495096797442049.

NAME 12: YOU ARE A NAME GIVER: RULING, BLESSING, AND NAMING

1. I learned this from an older mom, when I just had kids.

2. John F. Kilner, *Dignity and Destiny: Humanity in the Image of God* (Grand Rapids, MI: Eerdmans, 2015), 67, emphasis mine.

3. This example was inspired by a tweet from author Seth Haines (@sethhaines) on July 17, 2020, tweeting about his new experience in CrossFit.

4. Shared with permission.

5. Jürgen Moltmann, *Man: Christian Anthropology in the Conflicts of the Present*, trans. John Sturdy (London: SPCK, 1974), 1.

6. Ashlee Eiland, *Human(Kind): How Reclaiming Human Worth and Embracing Radical Kindness Will Bring Us Back Together* (Colorado Springs: Waterbrook, 2020), 52.

NAME 13: YOU ARE SENT: LIVING YOUR NAME

1. In *Garden City*, John Mark Comer asks a series of questions like these to get readers to consider their vocation. *Garden City: Work, Rest, and the Art of Being Human* (Grand Rapids, MI: Zondervan, 2015), 77–87.

2. In *Garden City*, Comer asks "What does your world need? When you look around at your city, your nation, your generation—the world at large— what is it that is missing?" (81).

3. Comer, *Garden City*, 84.

4. "Saltwater Kids," *Saltwater Sportsman*, July 2016, 22.

5. This quote was inspired by Dr. J. Robert Clinton's work, *The Making of a Leader: Recognizing the Lessons and Stages of Leadership Development* (Colorado Springs: NavPress, 1988), in which he asserts that God will develop a leader's ministry through various life stages, power and process items, checks, events, and boundary experiences over the course of their lifetime.

NAME 14: HE IS THE NAME ABOVE EVERY OTHER: THE NAME OF JESUS

1. David Bentley Hart, *The Doors of the Sea: Where Was God in the Tsunami?* (Grand Rapids, MI: Eerdmans, 2005), 86–87.

THE NAVIGATORS® STORY

———————— ◷ ————————

T HANK YOU for picking up this NavPress book! We hope it has
    been a blessing to you.

NavPress is a ministry of The Navigators. The Navigators began
in the 1930s, when a young California lumberyard worker named
Dawson Trotman was impacted by basic discipleship principles and
felt called to teach those principles to others. He saw this mission as
an echo of 2 Timothy 2:2: "And the things you have heard me say in
the presence of many witnesses entrust to reliable people who will
also be qualified to teach others" (NIV).

In 1933, Trotman and his friends began discipling members of the
US Navy. By the end of World War II, thousands of men on ships and
bases around the world were learning the principles of spiritual multi-
plication by the intentional, person-to-person teaching of God's Word.

After World War II, The Navigators expanded its relational ministry
to include college campuses; local churches; the Glen Eyrie Conference
Center and Eagle Lake Camps in Colorado Springs, Colorado; and neighborhood and citywide initiatives across the country and around the world.

Today, with more than 2,600 US staff members—and local ministries in more than 100 countries—The Navigators continues the transformational process of making disciples who make more disciples, advancing the Kingdom of God in a world that desperately needs the hope and salvation of Jesus Christ and the encouragement to grow deeper in relationship with Him.

NAVPRESS was created in 1975 to advance the calling of The Navigators by bringing biblically rooted and culturally relevant products to people who want to know and love Christ more deeply. In January 2014, NavPress entered an alliance with Tyndale House Publishers to strengthen and better position our rich content for the future. Through *The Message* Bible and other resources, NavPress seeks to bring positive spiritual movement to people's lives.

If you're interested in learning more or becoming involved with The Navigators, go to navigators.org. For more discipleship content from The Navigators and NavPress authors, visit thedisciplemaker.org. May God bless you in your walk with Him!

navpress.com

CP1308

God Sings a Louder Song
Than Suffering Ever Could

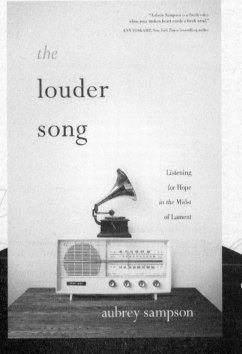

WHETHER YOU ARE DEALING WITH GRIEF, spiritual doubt, chronic pain, or a difficult season of life, there is a pathway through this suffering: lament. Lament anticipates new creation but acknowledges the painful reality of now. It recognizes the existence of evil and suffering—without any sugarcoating—while simultaneously declaring that suffering will not have the final say.

In your darkest times, let Aubrey Sampson help you discover that lament leads you back to a place of hope—because God sings a louder song than suffering ever could.

Available at NavPress.com or wherever books are sold.